the last seven pages

A Memoir of Hope

JAMES PINNICK

the

last

seven

pages

Print ISBN: 978-0-9960361-7-7
eBook ISBN: 978-0-9960361-0-8
First Edition 2014

Published in the United States of America

Cover design: Brian Ring / Brian Ring Design
Interior design by GreenE-Books.com

For Jennifer

ACKNOWLEDGMENTS

Thank you to Jason Chatraw, the first person who believed in the importance of publishing this message.

Thank you to Joy Neal for her endless amount of hours and dedication to the project.

A special thanks to Krystal Pinnick, Brian Ring and Rebekah Towers.

I'm grateful and humbled by your support.

TABLE OF CONTENTS

FOREWORD

I WALK DOWN THE CORRIDOR, my hands damp with anxiety. Is this really happening?

I remember all the times I've walked these floors to meet her for lunch. I hadn't really noticed the photographs lining the walls then, but now they seem to be closing in on me. Now I notice the details of the frames and the expressions on each of the portraits' faces. I want to stop and study each one, read all of their career titles, and delay my arrival at the end of this hallway as long as possible. Mostly I want to turn around and never come back here. It's too full of her living and working; it's too full of her sickness and dying. It's too full of her.

I see a group of people gathered at the end of the hallway, talking quietly. Never has fifty yards felt like such a formidable distance, but I come to the end and take my place with her colleagues and a few family members. They're all here to honor her life and work with a bronze plaque, which will grace the hallway I never noticed when she was alive and waiting for me at the end of it.

Jennifer loved her work as a nurse. Helping people and getting paid to do it was her calling and career tied neatly together. She had started in the medical surgical unit, transferred to telemetry, and then returned to the surgical unit where she felt most comfortable. She made her way through four different hospitals until she received an offer from the one right down the street from our new home in Phoenix, Arizona. During her time working here, patients and their families would write letters to the hospital about her.

"Jennifer took such great care of my mother. It was as if she were her own daughter," one began.

Another said, *"The patience that Jennifer had with my brother was wonderful. Even though my brother was an [—-] and a [—-] to her, she still treated him with dignity and respect."*

I knew this particular patient as "the punk" who continually returned her kindness with contempt. She kept her composure, remained professional, and showed him God's love.

As any family member or friend of a nurse knows, Jennifer's high standards for patient care didn't negate her right to tell anonymous stories about them. Once I put her call on speaker at work in order to multi-task, and everyone near my cubicle heard about the ninety-eight-year-old woman who passed gassed so loudly at night that the nurses heard it in their station four rooms down. "We thought there was an air drill in a construction area," she gasped out between laughs.

I miss hearing her tell stories, so I remember the ones she told me. There was the patient who continually muttered to herself about how much she loved blueberries, and who offered non-existent blueberries to anyone who entered the room. There was the guy who got a beer bottle lodged in his right eye over spring break, which still makes me cringe when I think of it.

I'm surrounded here by her colleagues, the management staff, family and the hospital CEO, who is telling everyone how impressed she was with Jennifer, and how she thought Jennifer would one day move up the ladder into management. I appreciate the acknowledgement of her capacity and potential, but I know she never would have taken a job in management. She didn't want any position that took her away from patients' bedsides. I speak a little, talk about my wife, and thank them all for coming. The ceremony is over in twenty minutes.

I step out of the frigid air conditioning into the late afternoon Arizona heat, and something inside me suddenly swelters and melts. I sit in my truck and cry. What do I have left of her? There are the people who know and love her, there are pictures and memories, and there's a plaque on a wall in the hospital. But it's not enough. None of it will ever begin to cover her absence in my life. The reality is starting to sink in, and I feel everything in me sinking with it. *I'm twenty-nine years old and I'm a widower.* I haven't quite faced this yet, but there it is hanging over me with such finality. It's unchangeable. Immutable.

But even as the reality of her death continues to settle, the story of God's faithfulness and transformative work over the past two years is starting to lift. There are people fighting for their lives who need to hear Jennifer's story. There are people who doubt God's presence in their darkest moments—Jennifer's story could reach them, too. There are people taking this day for granted while an anxious thought plagues them: *when I die, what's left?* Jennifer's story can meet them in those moments of doubt and spur them to begin shaping their legacies. A plaque can represent and commemorate, but it can't testify. I take a breath, start my truck, and drive home. I know what I need to do.

On March 28, 2009, breathing through a ventilator and unable to speak, Jennifer motioned for a pencil and some paper. For the last two days she spent on this earth, those pages were her voice—the voice of a young woman fighting with all her heart and soul. My most sacred possessions in this life are those seven pieces of paper, and they're a treasure I need to share.

Colossians 2:2

My goal is that they may be encouraged in heart and united in love… in order that they may know the mystery of God, namely, Christ, in whom are hidden all treasures of wisdom and knowledge.

PART 1

CHAPTER 1

I Need a Letter Shirt and a Cape

Saturday, March 28, 2009. Morning.

I HAD PRAYED IN THE SHOWER before driving back to the ICU and had a renewed hope that she was going to get through all of this. God was going to save her. I pulled reflexively into the garage with the shortest distance to the best parking, and then made my way into the hospital and back up to the dreaded eleventh floor.

A room in an ICU is a surreal, other world. I'm unfortunately very familiar with it but never became comfortable in it. Sometimes I felt like I was in a Michael Crichton novel. All this technology was about to do something wrong, and it would be my job to sort it out and be the hero. This particular ICU had a sliding door leading into each room, where medical equipment was stacked and crammed into every available spot. There was something beeping or blinking at me everywhere I looked. The odd 1950s-style window was the saving grace of this room—a glimpse into the outside world where we used to live.

I talked to the nurse before entering the room, and she told me that Jennifer had done well overnight. I asked questions, like, *when can she go home? How long will it take to regulate her breathing? When can she come off the ventilator?* But the nurse waved me in without answering. I wasn't ready to accept the answers to those questions.

I entered the room, walked straight to the side of her bed, and held the hand attached to a heart-rate monitor. Her eyes opened wide for a moment, then shifted back to normal.

"It's OK, I'm here," I said.

Her eyes rolled back and then returned to focus on the wall straight ahead, fully alert and conscious for the first time since her last surgery. She wanted to speak but couldn't because of the ventilator, so she slowly mimed the motion of writing. I found some sheaves of blank paper and a pencil in the nurse's station and saw Jennifer's smile grow as I approached with her requested tools.

"I love you. Where is everyone?" she wrote on the first page.

"No one wants to see you," I said. Her eyes rolled in response, and I noticed how tired they looked. She was tired of tests, tired of procedures, and tired of lying in a hospital instead of rushing from bedside to bedside as the caretaker.

"You did really well in surgery," I told her. "You're in the ICU at your old hospital because you had some trouble breathing last night. We're in the eleventh floor in room seven."

She picked up her pen again and wrote, *"I need a letter shirt and a cape."* I smiled.

She started to notice the pictures we had taped to the walls—Jennifer on horseback in a cute Gilligan's hat; the two of us scuba diving in Honduras; her beloved nephews; the two of us in Hawaii; Jennifer on the day she graduated nursing school.

As word got around to the waiting room that she was awake, family and friends began to filter in. Most noticed the pictures right away and studied them or commented on them. Jennifer kept her hand poised over the paper, interacting with people as they offered prayers and well wishes. I heard laughing and turned back to see where it had originated from. "What's so funny?" I asked. A friend pointed at Jennifer's latest note.

"If I can fight, pregnancy someday will be a breeze!"

I love her for looking to the future, for holding onto her dreams of being a mother, and for never letting go of God's promises for healing. One of the most haunting passages of scripture is Hebrews 11. The unnamed writer of Hebrews lists great people of faith—Abel, Enoch, Abraham, Isaac,

Jacob, Rahab—going on and on to list the multitudes of those who had believed God for great things and who held onto his promises. Then the writer concludes in one chilling verse, *"These were all commended for their faith, yet none of them received what was promised, since God had planned something better for us so that only together with us would they be made perfect."*

Her cousins had driven overnight from California and joined the room as friends from church also arrived. The nurses stretched the visitor limits until our room was full of people lending their love and support. Jennifer listened to their questions and participated in the conversation by nodding her head and writing notes. Then she brought the first page close and wrote a question in the center of it, asking all of her visitors to think about and discuss their favorite Bible verses.

Building relationships had always come as naturally as breathing to Jennifer. In fact, her capacity for facilitating relationships came even *easier* than breathing. Here she was struggling on a ventilator without a voice, and she was still bringing the people in the room together and driving the conversation to greater depths. People's answers spanned throughout the entire Bible, and soon we were reading and discussing scripture together.

My whole life as I know it is a testament to Jennifer's ability to reach out to others.

I was pretty secluded in high school. I was content with my regular table in the library and my few buddies. Jennifer was that *good* kind of popular—the kind that isn't maintained by looks or status. She simply weaved her way in and out of groups, was present with whoever was in front of her, and never used others to position herself. I knew her first as the girl who came to the library every day with a chocolate chip cookie.

One day, very unexpectedly, Jennifer simply walked over to my table in the library and started talking to me. I wasn't used to people talking to me for no apparent reason, but I also wasn't going to turn away attention from a girl. She came the next day and the next. "Did you have your chocolate chip cookie today?" she'd ask. I rarely said more than a word or two, but she kept coming. Sometimes she would place her cookie on top of my newspaper to get my attention. *What's with the cookies* I wondered in all my sophomoric depth.

Soon she started bringing two cookies—one for me and one for her. Once I teased that I really preferred warm cookies; she immediately stood up, walked over to the microwave, and warmed my cookie on high for fifteen seconds. I was sixteen years old and it was the sexiest thing a girl had ever done for me. Our first date was at a roller coaster park, our first kiss was in a car, and my mom taught me the box step before I took Jennifer to Homecoming. Our chemistry grew over actual Bunsen burners. It was a classic high school romance.

Looking back, I'm not sure what drove Jennifer to take

interest or reach out to me, as we didn't have all that much in common. She had a sibling and I was an only child. She had career aspirations while I had video games. She was lovely and intelligent; I was nerdy and reserved. She had a loving relationship with Jesus and I knew a man named Jesus who mowed my parents' yard. She was always reaching out to people, mentoring kids in her church, fostering relationships with people, and sharing God's message of love; I kept to myself as much as I could. I suppose I was just one of the many people she reached out to, and all those chemicals in chemistry class worked their magic and gave me a chance with her.

Throughout all of high school, I had no idea what I wanted out of life or who I wanted to be. I had decent grades and a thriving sports card trading business, but no real ambition or direction. Near the end of our senior year I asked Jennifer what she wanted to study in college. "I want to take care of people. I want to be a nurse," she said with a confidence that stunned me. I couldn't believe I was with such a strong woman who knew what she wanted out of life and how she would give back. I felt challenged to break out of my shell, but I didn't yet know how.

There in the hospital room on her second to last day, she was still showing me how. *Ask simple questions. Move the conversation outward and upward. Don't stay self-focused.*

As we were reading scripture and discussing our chosen verses, my Uncle Pat and his family joined us in the room.

After a few seconds of awkward silence, Pat decided he had a question to ask Jennifer about treatment. He took the pencil and paper from her hands and started writing, but Jennifer slapped his hand and took the paper back before he finished.

"What?" Pat asked, confused.

Jennifer pointed first at her ears, then her eyes.

"She can hear and see you just fine!" the room interpreted for her in unison.

In moments of great pain and sadness, the smallest sliver of light can be graciously blinding. The room erupted so loudly at poor Uncle Pat's mistake that a nurse came to see if something was wrong. He took it all in stride and settled into the atmosphere of support.

Another nurse came in to adjust some IVs and help Jennifer attend to some personal care, and the crowd moved quietly out of the room. When I came back in the room, I found a note to the nurse. *"Thanks for everything. You're gentle with my pain."*

It was my time to be alone with my wife. As I took a seat beside her, I stopped her from writing. "Just hang in there," I said, wanting her to relax after all the activity. I asked if she was in pain, and she shook her head side to side. "I love you," I said, and I didn't stop her from what she wanted to write next.

"I'm a little scared," she wrote on that first page.

Then she reconsidered and changed her message. *"I'm*

not scared. I just don't want to go." Her words hit me right to the core of my heart. She knew her body was shutting down.

I looked at my superhero wife connected to high-tech gadgets, relying on a strength that was both within her and far greater than her. She may not have been wearing a letter shirt and a cape, but she was unconquerable in my eyes. No matter the outcome, I knew she had won this fight. Jesus had won it for her, and she was persevering on the path set out before her. We just didn't know how many days, hours or pages she had left.

CHAPTER 2

I'm Still Alive

Saturday, March 28, 2009. Afternoon.

IN THE AFTERNOON she turned the first page over and placed a new sheet on top. After breaking her pencil tip, she easily could have decided that she was too tired and didn't want to write anymore. But she looked at her page and then up at me, down at her page and back at me, until I got the hint and brought her a new pencil.

The nurse stopped me in the hallway to ask if I wanted some lunch.

"No thanks, I'm not hungry," I lied. I didn't want to leave her room for any reason. I sat down beside her while she wrote.

"Did he remove any more cancer? Do I still have an obstruction?"

I focused on the pink eraser bobbing along as she wrote out the questions I didn't want to face myself, let alone answer for her.

"Will it ever go away? Can I fight this with more chemo?" She lowered the pencil and my mind struggled to focus and find the right words.

"You're always going to have to fight this," I said, finally. "I know it's your body, but I'm fighting alongside you. What else can we do but pray for the best?" The pencil slipped out of her hand and fell to the floor, and she snapped her fingers twice to signal that she wanted it back quickly.

"Just like old times," I joked. "Take out the trash! Do the dishes!" She smirked a little as she turned the paper on its side and wrote in the upper left corner.

"Yeah it sucks, but I'm still alive!"

A new wave of friends arrived, and the expression on her face turned joyful. The nurse walked in and asked where everyone had suddenly come from.

"They're a blessing from the church," she wrote to the nurse. And then to her friends, *"I know he hears all the prayers. I feel the prayers in my darkest hours."*

A family pastor was in the room, and he led us all in prayer right then. It was one of those moments when you could feel God's always-present Spirit in the room. I wanted to do something to mark the moment, so I turned to the pastor to ask a question.

"This isn't the way I envisioned this happening. But, Pastor, would you be willing to help us renew our wedding vows—right now?"

I sure know how to pick proposal locations. The first time was in a Las Vegas hotel bath tub, before Jennifer's renewed commitment to the Lord and my first commitment to him. We had been living together since college, and the Lord wasn't the only commitment that had me dragging my feet. Surrounded by bath bubbles on our weekend away, I finally asked her.

"Yes, I'll marry you," she said. "But I need to know you really love me." The doubts set in for both of us. *What if I screw this up?* I asked myself. *Are our differences insurmountable?*

After I proposed, we set about moving out of our apartment and buying a house. In our minds it was the next logical step in our relationship. If we were going to commit our lives to each other, surely we could commit to a house together. Perhaps we thought that the more we had in order before our marriage, the easier marriage would be. Now of course I realize that the only thing we really needed was a foundation in God's word and a community of believers to walk with us.

We were both still students, but we were well employed and had a growing joint savings. We furnished the house, and then we bought a cat that tore apart half our furnishings and a dog that shed on the rest. We golfed together and discussed starting a family after getting married—something we were both excited about. Jennifer worked hospital night shifts while attending RN classes in the morning, and on nights that I felt especially lonely without her, I'd load our golden retriever into the truck and surprise her at two in the morning with her favorite fast food. Then we'd lower the tailgate and eat under the stars together. We had such a good time in those stolen nighttime moments that it became a monthly tradition.

I worked for a credit card company during our engagement, and on September 11 of 2001, some of our employees were in the first building at Ground Zero. My job was to tell the families who were calling whether their loved one was accounted for or not. I answered six calls that day and still remember each one specifically. One was the mother of a young man who had just started work with us a week earlier. Another was a brother screaming inconsolably for his twin. Another man looking for his brother kept asking me what he should do next; should he go down there himself and look for his brother? I coached him to stay where he was and wait for word, but I didn't know what he should do or what I would do in his place. What do you do in moments when you have to do something but are absolutely powerless to do anything at all?

By the end of the day, I was completely drained. When I came home and shared everything with Jennifer, she listened carefully and then asked, "Did anyone you talked with want to pray?"

"I don't think so," I answered. "Why?"

"You should have offered to pray with them," she said. "If I was missing and my mom and dad were calling a hot-line, I would want the person on the other line to remind them God was in control." I still wasn't walking with the Lord at that time, and I had only ever prayed out loud during the World Series, but her words struck and convicted me. Jennifer always understood the power of prayer.

Sitting in the hospital room in that moment, I felt its power, too.

A hospital may not be the most romantic place to propose, but the questions we asked ourselves the first time had already been answered. Our love and commitment to each other was solid, and we had Christ as our foundation. The pastor agreed to my request, and I held Jennifer's hand and looked her in the eyes as we were led through the vows we had spoken five years before.

At our first wedding, the pastor forgot one thing. He didn't say, "You may now kiss the bride." We were so flustered with your typical wedding jitters that we didn't notice, either. It wasn't until we were outside being pelted with rice that our guests started shouting, "You never kissed her!" We stopped in the middle of the rice shower and kissed.

With the ventilator blocking Jennifer's mouth, I bent to kiss her head, and a family member snapped our last picture together.

"I love you, Jennifer," I said.

"I'm fighting this. I love you," she wrote.

A small line formed to pray with us, and each family member held Jennifer's hand so that she could feel the transfer of their prayers. There were tears in her eyes as the guests made their way through our receiving line—it was intoxicating to witness. Prayer is a powerful and potent tool. It not only allows us to communicate directly with God, but it binds together those who experience it. All who hear and participate are linked, lifted and filled.

After Hurricane Katrina hit in 2005, hundreds of victims were moved to temporary housing inside the Veteran's Memorial Coliseum near our home in Phoenix. Jennifer and I volunteered and were able to sit with people and listen to their stories. Jennifer also volunteered as a nurse and was able to participate hands-on in the healing process. Hearing the stories and being surrounded by people who had lost so much triggered an outpouring from my heart that I had never experienced before.

Jennifer and I spoke with one little boy who still stands out in my memory. He and his mom had lost everything in the storm, and the boy was carrying a toy car—the only one of his toys he had been able to take with him. They had come to Arizona with the hope that they could build a new life with the little they had and with their faith in God.

When Jennifer wrote, *"Yeah it sucks, but I'm still alive"* on the second page, I immediately remembered that boy and his mother. They lost everything, but they had so much hope and optimism for the future, because they relied on the Lord for strength and hope. As the outcome started looking more and more grim, I could see Jennifer leaning more into God for strength and hope.

Psalm 119:114

You are my refuge and my shield; I have put my hope in your word.

CHAPTER 3

Diving Above Ground

Saturday, March 28, 2009. Evening.

JENNIFER'S LOVE AFFAIR with the ocean started during an eighth grade trip to Catalina Island, which was the first time she put on a wet suit and tasted salt in her snorkel. From that first dive underwater on, she couldn't get enough of the sea: dolphins, fish, coral, seaweed, shells... she was fascinated with the underwater world.

In September of 2006 we went on our first scuba diving experience in Honduras. We weren't certified divers at the time, but we dove forty-four feet underwater into a beautiful reef. A grouper came up right beside me as if he wanted to chat and share some secrets, and I was filled with a sense of joy and adventure. But mostly I remember watching Jennifer have the time of her life. The day we swam with dolphins may have been the happiest I ever saw her.

From the corner of the hospital room, someone asked Jennifer a question about the respirator. "What's it like having that thing in your mouth?"

Jennifer picked up her pencil and wrote on a new piece of paper, *"Like scuba, but above water!"*

Of all the negative ways she could have described that machine she so desperately wanted to be detached from, I love that she chose to compare it to her favorite adventure activity. Scuba regulators can be really cumbersome in your mouth, but they're necessary if you want to see and experience life under water. And here was Jennifer, diving above water, fighting for her life.

When a nurse came to check on her, Jennifer wrote a request.

"Feeling better now. Pain under control. Can my tube come out?"

Around five in the evening, her request to have the breathing tube removed was granted. If it worked, she would come home again… I just knew it. If it failed, we stayed.

The procedure required four nurses and one doctor. They told her she would feel a lot of pain for about two seconds, and that she could yell. They would give her water and clean out her mouth, but she should be prepared for the pain.

I was standing in the waiting room when I heard her yell,

and all I could do was stand there and cry and sink into my helplessness. *Is this really happening?* I wondered for the millionth time. *Why?*

After a few minutes we were allowed back into the room. Jennifer was breathing under close monitoring, alert and looking around. But she couldn't speak—or didn't speak. We started to pray for improvement, for breath, for a miracle. Within ten minutes it was clear her vitals were starting to fail and that her body was in the process of dying. Before the procedure the doctor had asked me if I wanted the ventilator reinserted should she fail to breathe without it. *Yes,* I said, wondering why he had even bothered to ask. The team put the ventilator back in and attempted to calm her breathing. We were back to square one.

Once her breathing calmed, I asked her how she felt. She poked her thumb down. It had been an exhausting experience, both physically and emotionally.

The doctor came in and affirmed that her heartbeat was stable and that she would need to remain on the ventilator. Jennifer and I looked at each other and realized, without voicing or writing, that she would probably spend the remainder of her life diving above ground.

I stayed the night by her side, remembering a time when it was easier to picture our future…and how that all changed.

During our engagement we had become your typical DINKS—Dual Income, No Kids. We were in our mid-twenties and making over six figures between us; we had a small house payment, two vehicles, two pets and a timeshare. The market was in a great place when we decided to upgrade our home, and it sold for twice what we had paid for it. We moved in with family while our dream home was being built outside of Phoenix. Then, after a mortgage counselor talked some sense into us, we backed out of our agreement with the builder and hired a realtor instead. We looked at nineteen houses in three days and settled on a nice house in a great neighborhood outside of Phoenix. Some people complain about the lack of community in suburban towns, but we attended neighborhood barbeques, wine parties and block parties on a regular basis. Kids would trick-or-treat by the dozens on Halloween night, and we'd sit on the tailgate of my truck and pass out candy.

We continued on with life and our engagement, but after the dust of the new town and the excitement of new restaurants started to settle, things began to change. I'd often walk into a room and find Jennifer praying silently. I never knew what she was praying for, but for some reason it unnerved me.

Jennifer's faith had always been a part of her life, but it was starting to well up inside her more fervently. Meanwhile, I was still numb to that emptiness inside me. I knew some Bible stories from my childhood and thought they were just fine as far as stories go, but I was far more interested in watching sports with the dog than joining my wife in a Bible study. I also wasn't very communicative or open about our relationship, and our different work schedules made the problem worse. Jennifer told me that if I couldn't talk to her, I should start a journal that she could read when she got home. But I didn't even do that.

The chasm between us continued to widen, and her outbursts of tears became more frequent. We loved each other—even if I didn't fully know how to best show her my love—but as her faith began to deepen and widen, our drawn-out engagement and living situation was starting to tear her apart at the seams. I was self-centered and wasting my time away on things like computers and television and sports, while Jennifer was always there, inviting me into a more fulfilling relationship with her and the Lord. I was still a boy, and a rather shallow one at that. Jennifer needed a man of faith.

Maybe it was a weakness on her part that she chose to marry me; maybe she was scared because she didn't know life outside our relationship. Or maybe she had a peace from the Lord that surpassed the courage she could have mustered to go forward without me. In any event, we got married, we kissed under a rice shower, and we settled into our life as husband and wife.

I didn't worry about our marriage—I figured everything would just come naturally. I clearly see my naiveté now, but at the time I actually thought that marriage would just "happen." We would grow together, we would be happy together, and we would stay together. But the problems we had before marriage didn't disappear with a contract, and slowly I started to wise up to the fact that our relationship would require work. My first step was to start opening up more in conversation and begin writing in the journal she gave me. It was a miniscule step toward the foundation I needed for what came next.

In the summer of 2007, Jennifer started experiencing incredibly strong stomach pains. We assumed it was an ulcer, and she knew she needed to get it checked out. On an evening out with some friends, she excused herself from the table.

"Too many margaritas?" asked a friend of ours.

"I wish," Jennifer said. "I'll be back in a second." Then she locked herself in a restroom stall for what seemed like ages.

Two of her friends checked on her to make sure she was okay, but she sent them both back to the table. She eventually walked out of the bathroom and headed straight for the parking lot without explanation. I said goodbye for the both of us and tried to downplay the situation to our friends, but I knew something was very wrong.

"You okay?" I asked as I sat in the driver's seat.

"Everything inside me is swirling. It's like a bomb went off," she said. She promised to call for an appointment the next morning.

The doctor agreed that it was a bloody ulcer, prescribed her some antibiotics, informed her of the two week healing time, and sent her on her way. She picked up the prescription and we went out to a light dinner and movie to try and lighten her spirits.

After two weeks on the medication, Jennifer was still experiencing the same pains. She returned to the doctor twice over the next four weeks, and he prescribed two more rounds of antibiotics. Meanwhile I was researching her symptoms at work and "stomach cancer" kept popping up in my research. *Never do medical research online,* I thought, trying to assure myself. *You'll always think the worst when it's nothing.* I never told Jennifer what I was finding in my research because I didn't want to scare her. At nights the questions came at me in a whirlwind. *What if she has cancer? Would it be removed right away? What if it can't be removed? What would I do without her?*

Eventually the burning sensation in her stomach just wouldn't go away no matter what medication she took.

I was at work when the doctor called Jennifer with news from the test. I remember pulling up to the house, I remember walking in the door, and I remember the word changed everything for us.

"I have cancer," she said, and suddenly we were hugging and crying while I struggled to comprehend how a single word could shatter so much so quickly. This house, these dreams, this life, these plans—everything was lying in a puddle at our feet, as swiftly as if a glass of water had just slipped from her hand. By the time we went to bed that night we had already said everything there is to say out loud when the only thing you know is that it's cancer. *There will be options. You'll get treatment. We'll do what it takes.* Then we both stared at the ceiling in the dark, imagining all of the scenarios you imagine when the only thing you know is that it's cancer.

Her first oncologist appointment was scheduled for Monday, but by Friday—the day after the phone call—they had already decided she needed surgery as soon as possible. Friday was also the day that I opened the Bible for the first time in eleven years. I also emailed the pastor of the church on the corner to tell him we would be joining his congregation on Sunday morning, and he responded within several hours with a warm invitation.

It's rather unfortunate to make initial contact with a church on the same day that you're stealing moments to conduct internet research on your wife's stomach cancer. A foundation of faith and an established community of believers would have been so valuable at that exact moment in our lives. But that's how so many of us begin our walk with the Lord—in our dark moments, when we realize how much we've needed him all along. The skeptic would say we feel desperate and start grasping at straws for consolation. But I think it's because we're suddenly shaken from our apathy and begin asking the real questions that, had we asked them sooner, would have led us to the Lord sooner. I think our darkest moments can also be our brightest, because the answers we thought we had about life come up empty and begin to illuminate the questions that lead to truth.

I remembered to erase my internet search history that Friday so that Jennifer wouldn't see what I was doing. I read that 20 percent of people in her situation were alive after five years, and I was determined that she would be among them.

When Jennifer saw me open the Bible, she joined me for our first study together. We studied Philippians, which contained her favorite verse. *I can do all things through Christ who strengthens me.* What an incredible start. We decided to study together three times a week to get a better understanding of God and how he would have us navigate this season in our lives and marriage. I asked Jennifer if we should start from the beginning of the Bible, Genesis, and work our way through.

Genesis was boring. Genesis was getting us nowhere. I wanted to open the Bible and read verses that would calm the hurricane of questions and emotions we were facing, and I thought there were other ways that we should be studying the Bible that would be more productive. Maybe there was something else altogether that we should be talking about. I was wrong. The most important thing I could be doing was developing my foundation in the Word and my relationship with the Lord. The second most important thing I could be doing was developing my relationship with my wife. Both of those areas were being addressed in our study together, and I needed to stop looking for shortcuts.

That Friday night, the second night after the diagnosis, Jennifer rolled over in bed to face me. "I'm afraid to die, James," she said. "I don't want to leave you or my family. I want to become a mother more than anything—more than I wanted to become a nurse. I had a dream last night that I was holding our baby in this bedroom at the base of the bed, and I have to believe my dream."

I had to believe her dream, too. She cried herself to sleep in my arms, and a few minutes after she fell asleep, I rolled over and began crying. I pleaded with the Lord to heal her. Finally I turned my soaked pillow over to its fresh side and rolled back, placing my arm around her waist. She woke up briefly and turned to face me. Typically we both needed our space to sleep at night, but that night we fell asleep facing one another, hand-in-hand. As I fell asleep, I realized how badly I wanted answers, but that those answers weren't mine for the taking. And then an incredible, simple thought dawned on me: Maybe I couldn't know the answers, but I could draw close to the one with all knowledge and understanding. God—not the answers he held, but God himself—would have to be sufficient for me.

Neither of us wanted to get up on Saturday to face the day, but we slowly picked ourselves out of bed. I made breakfast out of oats that had been in our cupboard for two years and watched Jennifer sitting in her sun-stained chair by the pool, reading the Bible. Whatever revelation I'd had the night before wasn't rising to greet me this morning. I wasn't convinced that reading was going to help us. I finished my oatmeal and started tinkering around the garage for things to organize and donate, leaving her to read by herself. While working, I started dreading the thought of going to church the following day. Even though I had received a warm invitation from the pastor, I wasn't convinced the congregation would be as welcoming. How would they view us? Would they judge me for coming to church for the first time in the wake of a cancer diagnosis? Would they think I was insincere?

Sunday morning our dog, Chance, woke us up. We were planning to go to the evening service, which meant that our entire day became a clumsy attempt to get out the door to church.

"What should I wear?" I asked. Jennifer didn't know. Maybe the dress code had changed since she had last gone.

"Do we walk or drive?" It was a silly question since we could see the church from our doorstep, but we weighed the pros and cons of each before deciding to walk.

"What do we say when we get there?" We didn't answer that question. We just walked to church that evening in our best attempts at casual church clothes, trusting that we'd know what to say.

The church met in the student center of a college. The only way we had known it was a church was by the A-frame sign that we saw when we drove in and out of our block. How many times had Jennifer poked me in the ribs and said,

"Hey, we should check that out sometime"? That evening the pastor and his wife met us at the door and welcomed us, and we all exchanged greetings and names. We entered the lobby and browsed through the brochures before taking a seat on a couch in the back.

After a few songs, some announcements, a baptism and a sermon, we were standing in the back again. Jennifer remarked at how much she connected with the sermon—how she had read Romans 12 many times but never experienced or understood it that way before. Then she made some hot cocoa at the refreshment table in the back, which struck me as an odd thing to do in Phoenix in July, and we set about mingling.

That night we met people who would become some of our dearest friends. As Jennifer shared her story, other stories of cancer battles and survival came out, and I saw Jennifer lifted by the encouraging words of the people surrounding us.

We walked home that night witnessing a spectacular sunset—a gift of purple, Jennifer's favorite color. It was the first of many sunsets we'd experience together on our Sunday walks home.

The membership of the church was about a hundred people, which meant it was easy to meet nearly everyone at the church. After attending a few services, our new friends became more involved in Jennifer's story and needs. Some of the women in the church began to make and deliver meals to us in the evening during her treatments. Even later, when Jennifer would return to work, the meals kept coming. We were both overwhelmed at the constant deliveries at our doorsteps.

For the first time in my life I was fully engaged in a local church. I loved the music, the sermons and the people, but most of all I began to look forward to the time spent in prayer together as a group. I needed that time to stand with my brothers and sisters and go before the Lord with my prayers. As Jennifer got further along into treatment, she often wouldn't have the energy to stand for more than ten minutes. Many times I'd look down to see her crying and praying with her hands covering her face; I knew she was crying out to God to take away the cancer. It was in those saddest, most heart-wrenching moments that I began to feel God's love as a tangible presence in our lives. I was so grateful that he had taken away our dream house and led us through nineteen different homes until placing us next to this exact church.

On our walks home we would hold hands and discuss the sermon, feeling closer to God and each other with each passing week. The sunsets we saw were a spectacular gift from our Creator. We'd remark over the colors and watch for hints of that elusive purple that had covered the whole sky on that first walk home from church.

A week after she first received her diagnosis, we bought Chinese food and sat down to a conversation that neither of us wanted to have. We started by talking about treatments, and Jennifer said she hoped she might be able to avoid chemo if the operation was fully successful and if the newer pill treatments were appropriate. The questions got a little harder from there.

Do we stop making love because of the possibility of pregnancy?

Will God heal this?

Who do we tell?

Do we sell the house? Do we find a smaller place?

Should she avoid all treatments and just try to live out the remainder of her life free of toxins and unnecessary pain?

Jennifer worked through the answers, one by one. We would not hide any part of her disease—it wouldn't be fair to the people who loved her, and it would deprive her of the support she needed. Avoiding treatment was a legitimate question, but she answered it quickly. No, she wanted to come at this with any and all ammunition that seemed wise and reasonable. Financially, we trusted everything would work out, so we would stay put in our home. It was a difficult conversation, but we edged toward a hopeful realism, anchored in our belief that God was in control, whatever the outcome.

Jennifer became quiet for a moment. "If I die," she started, and I wanted to stop her immediately. *No, we're not going to talk about this*, I thought. But for whatever reason, I listened to her counsel me.

Don't be alone. Don't be afraid to remarry and raise a family.

Don't do anything stupid. (Don't kill yourself, is what she meant.)

Make sure my life insurance is in order.

Write. Write so that I can read your thoughts… write so that you can process this yourself.

Work to be successful. Success is not about money or power—it's about doing the things you were made to do.

Don't lose your faith. Live your life to honor God. Don't be afraid.

Her words of counsel continued, and as hard as it was, I listened. Then I made promises to her. Whatever she asked, I promised. It was just like her to put others first and look out for the people she loved.

At the end of that long night, we made one joint decision that would guide our day-to-day lives for the foreseeable future: We would avoid talking about cancer all the time, and would focus on living for the Lord. So much was out of our control, but we were taking ownership of the things we did have control over. We had a responsibility in how we would respond to this disease and interact with it on a daily basis. And while we wouldn't ignore the cancer, we wouldn't invite it to every meal, either.

When Jennifer described the ventilator as a scuba mask, I knew I was witnessing her taking ownership over her attitude toward her disease, even in her final hours. She desperately wanted to breathe without that mask, but she knew she would risk or lose her life if she did. Like a diver donning a mask to breathe underwater, she was choosing the equipment that would help her breathe, laugh, smile, write, and share God's love with every ounce of her final strength.

Joshua 1:9

Have I not commanded you? Be strong and courageous. Do not be afraid; do not be discouraged, for the Lord your God will be with you wherever you go.

CHAPTER 4

God Is Here with Us Now

Sunday, March 29, 2009. Morning.

JENNIFER WAS STILL ASLEEP when I woke up, and my phone registered several missed calls from friends who wanted to know whether she was in the same room as the day before. I gave my phone to my dad and asked him to field calls and visitors in the waiting room while Jennifer and I had some time together.

"What time is it?" she wrote to her nurse. *"Is James here?"*

"I'm right here," I answered. She turned toward my voice and then looked out the window. I could see the look of exhaustion on her face, which was the result of medicine continually flowing through her veins. But there was something stirring in her heart and soul as she reached for the fourth piece of paper.

"God is here with us now, I know."

I felt it too, before she even wrote the words. He was there. Of course, he had been with us throughout this entire journey.

After Jennifer's first surgery, we sat together and listened to the doctor tell us that the cancer was in its early stages. The surgeon had done everything he could do to scrape tissue and bacteria away from the remaining parts of the stomach, and it appeared that the cancer hadn't breached the stomach wall. Our family and friends roared with cheers.

After getting that report, I immediately went to the bathroom and sobbed. When the tears finally stopped flowing, I closed my eyes and offered a prayer of gratitude. Then I opened my eyes and saw six stalls and no urinals. I smiled at myself in the mirror, washed my hands, and left that women's room feeling peaceful.

Over the next six days of recovery in the hospital, people came by to visit and support her. But for as many people as we saw come through the doors to visit, I was surprised by a few of the faces we didn't see—people who were important to us. I came to understand that some people don't know how to react to tragedy and sickness and pain. Some family members drifted away and we lost a couple old friends; but we gained new ones, and many of the people we had met only once or twice at church came to visit. We had drawn near to the Lord, and now he was blessing us by bringing his people to us.

We came home from the hospital on a Saturday night, and Jennifer asked if we would go to church the next day. I told her we would go if she was able to walk. She said we could take the truck if she couldn't walk; I argued that the truck was too high and difficult for her to get into. I knew what I was trying to do even if I didn't understand it. Why was I feeling this resistance?

Jennifer wasn't feeling well enough to go on Sunday, but she kept asking me if I would go. Feeling pressured by the subtle pleadings of my sick wife, I went by myself and sat in the back of the church. It was my first time there without Jennifer.

During the second song, *Healing Rain*, something broke within me. If Jennifer had been there, I would have listened to that song through her ears only; I would have listened to the message that night hoping for words that might speak to her. But without her there, there were no ears to listen through but my own, and I felt God's healing rain pouring through my heart. It was the first time that I acknowledged and felt his very real presence with me. I went home and told Jennifer all about how I helped the crew tear down the sound equipment from the college facility, but I didn't mention my response to the service. That was something I wanted to share with her not through my words, but through the person I was becoming. I knew there was still a long road ahead for God's transformative work in me, but it was beginning.

I wasn't a natural-born nurse like Jennifer. The commitment for such care-giving service doesn't snap to attention and say, "Yes ma'am." It creeps in slowly, sometimes with ease, when love is present. For those who have given their lives to Jesus, I believe that presence is the Holy Spirit having influence over and in them. The Spirit of God witnessed my love for Jennifer, and it continually filled me and transformed me.

After a week of resting and recovering at home, we returned to the hospital to discuss further treatment options. I assured Jennifer that whatever the news or outcome, we'd make it through together. As I put the car in park, Jennifer asked if we could pray together.

"Definitely," I said.

"Lord, I just ask you to take away my pain," Jennifer began. "I was up all night. I ask you to heal me starting today." She started to cry. "Please, please Lord, touch my body and heal me. In your name we pray, Amen."

I wanted to offer more reassurance. "The doctor will be discussing treatment options today, but it is God who knows his plans for you," I said, not even certain that what I said made sense. We got out of the truck that we had filled with our prayers of hope and walked into the office, where were told to wait in the room four doors down to the left.

"Lucky number seven," I said with a smile when I

noticed the room number.

Our anxious hands remained interlocked. We were a team.

Jennifer's primary care physician was out of town, which we knew going into the appointment. We were disappointed about it, but we wanted the referral we needed as soon as possible.

The doctor on call came into the room, sat down, crossed her legs, and started to type away at her laptop without even greeting us. She started to get frustrated with the balance of her computer, then finally uncrossed her legs and continued typing on a stable surface.

Wow, was all I could think.

Jennifer and I looked at each other and remained patient, waiting to see how the conversation would begin. After a few more awkward moments, the doctor looked directly into my eyes.

"What are your plans for treatment?" she asked.

Jennifer and I were both caught off-guard. *My plans?* I wondered what she could possibly have been reading and typing if she didn't even know the person with cancer was a female. I hesitated for a moment.

"You're supposed to tell us," I said. "You're supposed to give us a referral. And it's my wife who needs treatment, not me. Why aren't you prepared to see us?"

The doctor was unaffected by my response and merely turned a few degrees to face Jennifer.

"What are your plans for treatment?" she asked, as if these were her first words.

Jennifer explained that she was diagnosed with cancer, that she'd already had surgery, and that she was now there to discuss additional treatment options.

Absolutely nuts! I raged inside.

The doctor looked down at the report in front of her. "Yes, you have cancer," she said.

That was it. I told the doctor to leave the room immediately, and I went to the front desk to demand a different doctor—any doctor but the one we had just seen. It didn't matter to me whether insurance covered the visit or not; I just knew I never wanted to see that physician again.

When the next doctor came in the room, I was still livid. I ranted about the idiocy of the previous doctor. "She didn't have the simple tasks down," I fumed. "She was so rude! She had no right to be a physician." I calmed down after a few minutes, and we discussed what we had actually come to discuss. When the doctor left the room, Jennifer and I sat a little while longer and prayed. God was there with us even in our anger and frustration.

Driving home we flipped through radio stations and came across a new Christian music station we hadn't heard before. Our spirits lifted a little higher.

Two weeks later we were back in the truck headed toward the hospital for her first chemotherapy treatment. In my mind—which was still scared of and unaccustomed to illnesses—I would wait in the aptly-named waiting room, ready to drive her home after the procedure. It wasn't until we were sitting in the waiting room and I saw a couple leaving the office together, hand-in-hand, when I realized what I was doing. *How pathetic are you?* I asked myself. *You can't go in with your wife? Suck it up!* I had to go in; I had to be there to make her laugh, to hold her hand, to support her. My desire to draw back was continually being transformed by the Holy Spirit. I was leaning in.

Jennifer's oncologist was a Christian man who knew Jennifer from her days working at that hospital. He greeted her with a hug, then took our hands and prayed with us. What a blessing to have a doctor welcome the Lord into the room with us. This doctor was honest about the aggressiveness of the cancer, provided a set schedule for treatments, and answered some of our most difficult questions.

"Is this going to work? How long do I have to live?" Jennifer asked.

It's a rare gift to be able to speak truthfully, sincerely and hopefully about a difficult situation, but our doctor had that gift. He explained that Jennifer had a fast-moving cancer, but that the medical team would help Jennifer fight it by any means necessary. Then he reminded us that God was in control, and everything was in his hands. He didn't claim to be the judge of time, but we knew things were serious by the aggressiveness of the schedule he set before us.

For the first couple weeks, the chemo didn't seem to

have an effect on Jennifer. Then the nausea started to set in. On the way home from one of her treatments, she asked me to get off the freeway several exits before ours. I sat in the car feeling completely helpless while she was sick. When she got back in and closed the door, I was struck by the fact that she had to this all over again in two days. It was too much.

Over the next two months of treatment, I saw her change. As her body began to weaken, her spirit grew in strength and determination. While so much of what was happening to her body was out of her control, she retained control over her mind and heart. Her oncologist wanted to throw in a double session of chemo one day for good measure: done. He increased the chemo dosage after two weeks, telling her it would cause more nausea and light headedness: done. Jennifer was there to work and she wanted to live. I saw hope for the future build behind her beautiful brown eyes. Every day that she went to chemo was another day marked off on her treatment calendar. She marked the last day of treatment on the calendar with simply a smiley face.

Meanwhile, I was losing all of my focus at work. I finally told my boss exactly what was happening, and the empathy and understanding I received was overwhelming. But I couldn't concentrate or communicate as well as I had before, and I was forgetting simple tasks. I'd spend much of my morning researching all of the new medical terms that had been thrown at Jennifer during her appointment. One thing was becoming clear: Jennifer's prognosis was not good. Despite all the positive talk and determination on everyone's part to help my sweet wife, the statistics were downright miserable.

After chemotherapy came radiation. Unlike the hospital thirty minutes away where she received chemotherapy, her radiation treatments took place at the hospital where she worked just three miles down the road. Some of her nursing colleagues from the fourth floor would stop by the waiting room to say hello and to encourage her. Her treatments were scheduled for twenty minutes a day, four days a week, for six weeks. I would watch as she lay in that dull room with a machine localized over her lower-right side. She would feel a burning sensation inside, and over time the skin in that area developed a sunburned color. Now she was constantly nauseated, and even though the hospital was only three miles from home, we never made it back without stopping. At night she slept on her right side so as not to irritate the burn that was being constantly renewed with each treatment.

After her first three treatments, I knew she needed a surprise. I came home from work with three dozen roses hidden behind my back, and grabbed her left hip to turn her towards me. She cried out in pain, and I realized I had grabbed her burned side. Despite her pain, she accepted the roses with gratitude. And she continued to accept the treatments, knowing they were the key to this fight.

Soon after both chemotherapy and radiation treatments

were complete, Jennifer returned to work. She had wanted to return earlier, but the doctors wouldn't clear it. We worked together to improve her stamina by doing some light hiking in the mountains and walking around town. Twelve-hour nursing shifts require a lot of energy, even for a well person.

Over the next year she seemed to be doing great at work. She would occasionally excuse herself and deal with her continuing nausea, and her boss gave her four patients instead of the usual six. But everyone knew that she wanted to make a difference in people's lives, and no one seemed to mind picking up a little extra work to support her. Throughout that year she settled into something that resembled normalcy. She was maintaining her nursing career, investing time with her family and friends, and attending church and small groups with me. We continued our Bible studies together as well as our midweek fellowship group, which was greatly beneficial to both of our growing walks with the Lord. Going to church on Sunday was one thing, but actively delving into the Word with other believers while sharing our hearts and prayers with them was what grounded our faith and propelled us forward.

The one missing piece, we decided, was a child.

We had begun trying to have a baby several years before cancer, and while each of us had come out clear in fertility tests, it just didn't happen. When the cancer diagnosis came, we decided to prevent pregnancy so that we could focus our attention on her healing.

After the first surgery, when the prognosis seemed good and we were filled with hope, we resumed our attempts to have a baby. The doctors assured us that the chemotherapy and other treatments posed no threat to getting pregnant or a baby in the womb. When we were again unsuccessful, we decided to attempt an adoption. Eight weeks into the process, we were denied on account of Jennifer's cancer diagnosis. We hadn't expected that outcome, but we understood and accepted it. Jennifer's biggest dream in the world was to become a mother, and one of the reasons I married her was because I knew what an incredible mother she would be. The fact that we didn't leave any stones unturned or put those dreams on hold gives me peace that it was simply not meant to be. God knew better.

One warm Phoenix night in September, I felt everything catching up with me at once—my wife's sickness, our hopes and disappointments over starting a family, and the growing pains in my faith and spiritual transformation. I decided an evening swim in the pool might be the refreshment I needed. After slipping in the pool and centering myself on our green raft, I turned over on my back and closed my eyes.

"Lord, if you can hear me," I said into the night air, "I'm scared out of my mind. I'm lying on a raft of all places, praying for you to guide us." I looked up and saw the formation of the stars and felt God's presence fill the night surrounding me. All at once in that moment, I fell completely in love with Jesus. I knew he was present. I laid there resting in my new awareness and peace. Then I heard the patio door open and saw Jennifer poke her head out. "Are you coming inside? You'll get all wrinkled up!"

I slid off the raft and made my way toward my beautiful wife, all the while thanking God for his love and assurance. We weren't alone. God was with us. I knew it.

Psalm 139:10

… even there your hand shall lead me, and your right hand shall hold me.

CHAPTER 5

Am I Doing Better Than Yesterday?

Sunday, March 29, 2009. Afternoon.

AFTER ONE FULL DAY in the ICU, Jennifer's left hand started to throb. It could have been from gripping her pencil too often or simply from the medicine reaching her extremities. She persevered. She kept writing. Friends from our church arrived with more smiles and well-wishes; nurses filtered in and out. When one came to draw blood from her bruised and painful arms, Jennifer wrote, *"I don't mind the pokes. I'm a fighter."*

The surgeon came in earlier than expected to check Jennifer's status.

"Am I doing better than yesterday?" she asked, barely able to

complete the sentence.

The doctor didn't provide a substantive response, and as he left I noticed Jennifer was changing for the worse. She was no longer laughing, smiling, or blazing fire with her pencil. She started to drift in and out of sleep.

Some of the best "yesterdays" I had with Jennifer were during her remission. In those bright, hopeful five months following treatment, we thought she might be beating the odds. It seemed that way, anyhow. Fresh out of such a hard season and inspired to make the most of every day, we went on two trips. The first was Disneyland—truly one of Jennifer's favorite and happiest places on earth. I watched her skip down the road in her Mickey Mouse ears and ride the teacups many times in succession. Disneyland erases the years since youth, and most importantly, it erased that one difficult year of cancer. It was a perfect celebration.

On our long, peaceful drive home from California, we started planning our trip to Hawaii.

Hawaii had always been a bucket list item for Jennifer and me, and we knew it was time to take it off the backburner and make it a reality. We spent the next couple months doing little more than saving for our trip and carefully planning each of our seven days on Kauai. We took a scuba certification class at our local YMCA, which was a great chance to spend time together, gain a new skill, and actively look forward to Hawaii, where we would perform the four open dives required for certification.

Throughout all the saving, planning, researching and dreaming, there was one thing we knew for certain. Cancer was not invited on this trip. We would go to Hawaii, come hell or high water, and we would leave cancer behind for seven days.

We arrived in wet, sticky Kauai after a short puddle-jumper flight from Honolulu, rented a red mustang convertible, and drove past green-covered mountains on muddy one-way roads. By the time we got to our hotel, the car was covered in mud. Jennifer had rolled her window up and down throughout the trip, poking her head out to soak in the tropical air while estimating how long it would take to roll up the window before the next mud puddle ahead. Sometimes she miscalculated and would have to wipe the mud off her glasses. It was on that ride that I knew we had been successful; cancer was nowhere in sight.

Our hotel was a mere ten yards from the ocean, and at night we had to keep our patio door closed to keep the ocean from splashing us in bed. On our first day we lounged around on the beach and got properly sunburned and ocean-soaked. We ate shaved ice from a vendor and alternated between taking cover from the rainstorms and enjoying the cloudless views of the mountains. We drove back to the airport we had just come from for a helicopter tour—an extravagantly fun way to get our bearings on the island. We bought groceries at a Walmart in paradise and ate dinner in our room with the door open to the breeze. Jennifer had often been cold during chemo, but here she was basking in warmth. (Personally I prefer a little air conditioning, but I kept my mouth shut.)

The next day we zip-lined between trees, working our way from short distances and small heights to longer lines and steeper falls. I watched in amazement as Jennifer swung around the forest in her harness, completely free. Later that day we watched the sunset and walked the beach at a posh, five-star hotel. Jennifer found a huge conch shell and wanted to keep it, but she needed to smuggle it through the hotel first. We walked into the hotel in our zip-lining clothes and did our best not to appear out of place among the dressed-up guests. Jennifer stuck the stinky conch shell under her shirt as we stood in an elevator with several other people, and we both pretended we didn't notice the horrible smell.

Back at our hotel we emptied the conch shell so that it could dry overnight. We washed it out in the bathtub and scrubbed it with laundry detergent... all with no success. Our room smelled horrendous, but Jennifer loved the shell and wouldn't get rid of it. We went out for dinner and ate crab and lobster, and then returned to the hotel and stuck the shell outside for the night.

We went up on another flying tour—this time by an ultra-light airplane—and flew between canyons and mountains, over valleys and above white-sand beaches. We flew just above the coast, almost skimming the water, and then again high above the rainbow vistas, stealing glances at each other all the while. Could this really be happening to us? It was spectacular. At one point Jennifer saw dolphins jumping out of the water, and her expressions were so priceless that I hardly wanted to look away from her to see the dolphins myself. She rated the experience among the top five in her lifetime.

Though the stench of the conch shell followed us throughout our trip, we didn't sniff even a hint of cancer. We just kept diving, zipping, flying, snorkeling, eating and walking along the beach, hand-in-hand. On the day we completed our fourth dive and graduated as certified divers, we high-fived each other as proud desert folk with oceanic accomplishments.

Despite all of Jennifer's best efforts, the shell still stank on the day of our return. She triple-wrapped it in a sweater and somehow got it through security in her checked bag. At the baggage claim in Phoenix, we knew Jennifer's bag by the smell before we even spotted it. Once home, Jennifer washed all of her clothes three times and eventually threw out one of her sweaters. But the smell was growing fainter, and the shell found a place in our home. Over time it stank less and less, until it became a lovely, odorless memento of our trip. I hope time never does to my memories of that trip what it blessedly did for that conch shell. I want every sight, scent and moment to be recorded in my memory forever.

One month later, shortly after my birthday, Jennifer's reflux returned.

"It's here again," she confided in me one terrifying night. "I don't want more chemotherapy. I don't want more surgery." She made an appointment with her doctor.

With high hopes but low expectations, we went to a new surgeon for a new opinion. The results of the scan were devastating. Cancer was back, and Jennifer needed the remaining ten percent of her stomach removed, followed by more chemo. We walked out of the hospital in shock.

Late into that night I listened to her whisper into her pillow, pleading with the Lord. I rolled over and did the same, bargaining my life for hers, asking God to stop my heart and give her a full life. God heard my prayer but he didn't answer me. He was there and he didn't give us what we asked. But he was there, and somehow that was enough.

Jennifer went into surgery a couple weeks later knowing that the freedom and quality of life she had been enjoying until now were in jeopardy. She felt stuck between the grief she was feeling and the need to forge ahead.

The surgery was supposed to take four hours but instead took six. We knew this wasn't good news, but continued to receive reports that all was going well.

While Jennifer was in recovery, the surgeon came out to speak with us. We knew by his face that things were grim. He made no attempts to maintain a detached exterior, but instead leveled with us, emotion painted all over his fatherly face. The surgery had been successful in an artificial way, he explained, in that he removed everything (and more) that he intended to remove. But the cancer was aggressive, and had she been an older woman, he would have closed her up without bothering to remove anything at all. There would be no cure. Jennifer would die from this disease.

How much more could she endure, I wondered? *All of it, by the grace of God,* I knew. Despite my anger, I knew God wasn't toying with her. I knew she was his. He was holding her in his hands and watching her align her will and desires with his. He was gently guiding her, showing her the way through the pain.

Life is a gift that always ends in death. The question isn't, "How long do I get to spin around on this blue orb?" It's, "What am I going to do with my turn?" We shouldn't be like children who cry when it's time to get off the carousel; we should feel grateful for what we were given. *But I want to go again—I don't want to stop,* we cry. *That was the turn. That was your gift.*

The one burning question I had to ask was how they could take so much out of her body and still not have gotten all of the cancer. My eyes were so flushed with tears that I couldn't see and my shirt was soaked through. With Jennifer alone in the recovery room, I didn't need to be the rock. I cried until I was hyperventilating and needed to leave the room. Later I returned and sat next to my dad, who put his arm around me. I cried under the safety of my dad's arm, knowing I would in fact be losing my wife. I stayed at my parents' house that night.

When Jennifer was alert enough to talk the next morning, we chose our words wisely. The doctor told her the facts of the matter, which sounded more optimistic than they were. He didn't see any cancer at the moment, but he recommended more chemotherapy. Jennifer was a nurse, and maybe she read between the lines further than we hoped. But she needed the encouragement to keep going.

Friends and family came by her room with cards and flowers. Her energy level was pretty remarkable for the first few days after surgery, and she started on her new diet of puddings and shakes. Her body naturally developed a new space for her food in place of a stomach, and she could handle small portions of solid food. She began chemotherapy again.

While the doctors hadn't given her any solid details on her life expectancy, I think she knew at this point that she would live the rest of her days with cancer and treatment. Whether she knew how brief that time would be or not, I can't be sure. But she was accepting everything as it came and dealing with her sorrow and grief as it came, too.

Chemotherapy was a different experience this time around. She started to really look like a cancer patient, as she lost both hair and weight at a rapid pace. She refused to wear a wig, scarf or hat and decided to spike what was left of her hair, which looked really stylish on her.

One Monday night I was preparing dinner while watching football when I heard her scream at the top of her lungs, and it occurred to me that she had just seen her first scorpion. She hated spiders and the like, and we happened to live in an area known for scorpions. As I turned the corner to enter the bedroom, I heard the water shut off and the shower door open; I could see her bending down, trying to pull something from the bottom of the shower floor.

"It'll bite you back if you stick your hand down the drain," I said light-heartedly. She turned to me with a towel over her head and tears in her eyes, and she slowly covered herself with another towel. She stepped out of the shower and dried off, silent.

"How big is it?" I asked, a little gentler now that I saw how upset she was.

"The water won't go down," she answered.

"Just crunch it with the shampoo bottle and it'll drain," I said.

My eyes focused on the shower floor for the first time, and I saw the water had started to flow over the edge of the stall. I reached into the soapy water with my hand and felt the top of the drain, but I couldn't feel anything. I returned with my screwdriver and popped the steel top off, then reached in and felt something soft. I pulled out a handful of hair, then another. My heart sank with the water. I was a fool.

"Thanks for fixing the drain," she said, removing the towel on her head in front of the dresser. I went back into the bedroom and approached her from behind, wrapping my arms around her waist and kissing her head, now almost bald.

"Are you okay?" I asked softly.

"Thanks for the drain, James," she repeated as she walked out of the room.

I passed by the shower again and saw her wet footprints on the carpet—one set in front of the shower and the other directly in front of the mirror. I put the scene together in my mind. She must have gotten out of the shower when she noticed her hair falling, shrieked, and then returned to finish her shower. I prayed that she hadn't felt alone. I hope she drew near to God in the shower and felt his presence as surely as the water rushing over her.

Psalm 3:4

I sought the Lord and he answered me; he delivered me from all my fears.

After the second round of chemotherapy, Jennifer had to be drastically cautious about what she ate, as much of it didn't agree with her. She continued to swim in our pool for fresh air and light exercise, using sunblock to protect her overly sensitive skin and a hat to protect her scalp. In some ways life returned to normal again. She continued to work for a few months and no longer had the chemo port in her chest. But she wasn't in remission. She knew that.

After a couple of uneventful months, she became a patient in her own unit when she developed pneumonia. Her lungs were drained by a small hole in her back.

The day after she was admitted, everyone from our Bible study came to study with us in the hospital room. The nurses turned a blind eye to the visitor limits as a dozen people crammed into her room and began lifting up Jesus' name and praying over Jennifer. At one point I had to step out of the room to compose myself, but I returned as quickly as possible, not wanting to miss that beautiful moment of Christian unity.

During a follow-up meeting, the doctor who had prayed with us before beginning her first round of chemotherapy gently told us that he would not be treating Jennifer any more. He was transitioning to palliative care, meaning that he would do whatever he could to relieve suffering. Further chemo wasn't going to help, and he wouldn't provide it. "I'll do whatever it takes," Jennifer said, but there wasn't anything left to do.

She asked how much longer she had, and he reminded her that the timing was in God's hands. She didn't demand a different response. She would allow her faith to rise in place of certainty.

Once home we attempted to return to our normal married life, but Jennifer had digressed to the point that intimacy as we had known it was no longer an option. That didn't stop me from loving her. I held her hand and wrapped my arms around her and said things to make her forget she was a cancer patient.

One night I heard her in the bathroom, crying. I sat

outside the door, trying to respect the fact that she had closed herself in that solitary space for a reason. But while I could respect the space she wanted, I couldn't leave her alone. I sat with my back to the door, thinking about all the times in the previous years I had wished for a barrier from the hard work of marriage. But this was no moment of cowardice. We both needed that door. Neither of us was strong enough to hold the other in the moment, but with something strong between us, anchoring us, we could lean on one another. The Lord had been like this door throughout our entire journey. Neither of us had been strong enough to hold up the other, but with the Lord Almighty between us, we had never fallen. I asked her where I should book our next hotel, and Jennifer's spirits lifted as she started talking about our vacation and Saturday night plans and even Christmas.

When Jennifer asked her doctor if she was better than yesterday, the unspoken answer was no. She was not better in any measurable sense. But by God's grace she was ever closer to his glory. We were both being continually perfected in his love. We were far, far better than yesterday.

Proverbs 4:18

But the path of the righteous is like the morning sun, shining ever brighter until the full light of day.

CHAPTER 6

He Came to Me Through Faith in Him

Sunday, March 29, 2009. Afternoon.

I DON'T KNOW WHEN and where I'll prepare to meet my King, but I can only hope I'll do so with half the strength, courage and hope that Jennifer displayed in her last hours. By this time, cancer had nearly consumed her body, and her eyes were beginning to stay closed on a more consistent basis. I looked up and saw her grabbing for the pencil and looking for another sheet of paper, her sixth.

"He came to me through faith in Him," she wrote.

She could barely get through the sentence, but I marveled at where she had summoned the energy. At first I thought it was a reference to a specific Bible verse, but it wasn't—it was just her, writing what came from within her heart. God is not silent; he is still speaking to us. She was communicating a revelation.

Two months prior to these days in the ICU, we had thrown a Super Bowl party at our house to celebrate our favorite team, the Cardinals. We had two televisions playing at the same time, one broadcast and one satellite. There was a three second delay between the two, so half the party would hear the reaction from the other room before seeing the play. Jennifer deemed it our best party ever. Her hair was almost entirely gone and she was very sick, but she was mobile and stable.

The next month, February, found Jennifer still struggling with her eating and digestion issues but otherwise emotionally confident and positive. She found ways to celebrate what had once been the most common of activities, like waking up in the morning, walking, relaxing, and going to bed with me at night.

By the beginning of March, things changed. She didn't have the energy to walk around and she slowly lost her desire for mobility. Socializing with friends, once her favorite activity, became tedious and difficult. When friends came over, she stayed on the couch. She felt like she was losing her identity to this illness, and I, too, started to see her as a sick person. It scared me to see the woman I loved diminishing right in front of me.

My boss had long since given me all of the freedom and

flexibility I needed to work from home, and she also offered grace and understanding when I didn't accomplish the very little that was expected of me. But after a while I couldn't continue to accept her leniency towards me. It just didn't feel right. I couldn't focus on my work, as any time I had on my laptop was sacrificed to obsessively and compulsively researching care options for Jennifer. I knew it was only right that I officially leave my job.

Jennifer had quit working in June of 2008 but was still on payroll through Life Event Status, so we switched over to her insurance and lived off our savings. The bank wouldn't work with us in modifying our mortgage, so we planned on ruining our credit score and going into foreclosure after twelve months. Our finances weren't anywhere on the list of our concerns.

James 5:13-14

Is any among you sick? Let him call for the elders of the church, and let them pray over him, anointing him with oil in the name of the Lord.

Before she was hospitalized for the final time, our pastor and five elders from the church laid hands on Jennifer as she sat crying and praying for God to remove her cancer, her fears and her anger. I sat in another chair to her right and held her hand, praying with the rest that God would heal her.

After the anointing service we slowly walked home, hand in hand. As usual, I walked with my head down so that Jennifer would be the first to look west and glimpse the sunset. She broke her grip with my hand and stopped in her tracks.

"Is everything okay?" I asked.

"I know he's with us," she said, pointing to the waves of clouds in the sky. My gaze met the brilliant purple sunset.

"It's written all over the sky," she said. "Can't you see his writing?"

The sixth page is very simple: Jesus comes to us through faith in him. All of us who put our hope and faith in him are promised an eternal life that can't be tainted by sickness and pain. We wanted that promise right now; we had pleaded with the Lord to grant it. Instead he made it clear to us that he was present with us in Jennifer's suffering. He showed us that his presence, not his healing hand, was what we most desperately needed. When you give your life over to Jesus, he comes running with open arms and his love written all over the sky.

Jeremiah 29:13

You will seek me and you will find me, when you seek me
with all your heart.

Jennifer's final surgery was the beginning of her earthly end.

Around March 26, she could no longer drink water and became dehydrated. There was a blockage in her esophagus and surgery was necessary. The next day she was connected to an IV and prepped for surgery. Friends and family gathered, and we all knew what was at stake. If the blockage was cancer, that would be the end. If it was an intestinal blockage, it could be removed.

The operation lasted six hours. When it was over, I came into the room where Jennifer was lying in bed, struggling for a little bit of air, her mouth covered with tape with the ventilator attached. I tried to help calm her down until her heartbeat settled. Then her surgeon approached us with the results of her surgery, confirming our worst fears. He couldn't remove the blockage, as it would have killed her immediately.

People often ask, "Why do good things happen to bad people?" When you're watching your young wife poised for death and gasping for air, this is the only question you can ask. And none of the answers, no matter how logically or theologically or philosophically sound, are good enough.

Eventually Jennifer calmed down and caught her breath. With each stable rise and fall of her breathing chest, my denial returned and dug itself further in. She would be okay. She would be transferred to the ICU to get better. That night, despite my protests, the nurses and my family convinced me to go home and sleep. I hadn't slept more than a couple hours at night for some time, and I guess it showed.

***

The sixth page is the greatest treasure that Jennifer ever left me. I took it to a tattoo artist to have some sketches made, and then placed the page in the console of my truck where it sat for a few days and suddenly disappeared. I remembered cleaning out my car, and I hoped and prayed that it hadn't made it into a stack of papers that I threw away. I searched every moving box and hamper and drawer in my home—nothing. When I realized that it was likely lost to me forever, I cried. With how carefully I had cataloged of all of Jennifer's items, it baffled me that I could so carelessly misplace the one I treasured most.

Now I see how fitting it is that this most important page is out of my reach. It's like Jennifer in that way. My greatest treasure on earth is now just a memory, blessed and sacred.

CHAPTER 7

I Want to Go Home

Sunday, March 29, 2009. Afternoon.

AS SHE CONTINUED to drift in and out of sleep, Jennifer gained one last surge of strength and clarity. She took a deep breath, let out an even deeper sigh, and picked up her pencil. The moment was in slow motion, as if already a memory.

"I want to go home."

The sentence is scrawled in nearly perfect penmanship at the top of the seventh page, where it stands alone.

At the time I understood the message as I wanted to believe it, thinking that she wanted to return to our Phoenix home and resume our life together. But pushing against my deep sense of denial was the truth. She had accepted what was happening and was coming to a place of peace and even longing. She wanted to go to her true home.

The doctors came in with more options to extend her life in the sort of miniscule way that we had until this point, which always involved more holes and procedures. I sat down in a chair and pressed the palms of my hands against my eyes. I knew the decision in front of me but needed a sense of assurance about it, so I went to her bedside and took her hand in mine.

"Jennifer, your body is not helping you right now," I said, my voice breaking. "I need to know if you want to see Jesus. Please squeeze my hand if you would like to go see Jesus."

I never felt a squeeze. I only remember her soft skin that left an imprint my hand will never forget. The message at the top of the seventh page would be her last.

Later I entered her room again to find a hospice representative waiting for me. She led me to a room where our families were waiting, and I edged my way to a seat in the back of the room. The nurse handed some pamphlets and brochures to everyone, and then she handed me a form printed on a red piece of paper. The acronym DNR—Do Not Resuscitate—glared at me from the top of the page.

"I feel like I'm killing her by signing this," I said, blind from tears.

"No, James," our families assured me unanimously. "You're releasing her from her suffering."

I heard my mother's voice speaking slowly and patiently to me, like I was still a child. "She would do the same for you, James," she said.

My hand could not grasp the pen, and I prayed for strength. I opened my eyes, took the pen, and started to write my name. But I couldn't finish. My pen was shaking and the paper was wet from my sweat. It took me a minute to finish signing the name I usually scribbled so casually and quickly in matters of no importance. With each loop and curl of the ink, my brain screamed at me from all directions. *I don't know! Is this right? Am I killing her?* In the end I managed to finish my signature by convincing myself that she would be the one to get out of hospice alive. All she needed, I decided, was a peaceful environment for her body to begin repairing. I handed the form to a nurse, who informed me that the staff would remove the ventilator per my instructions, and that Jennifer would be moved to hospice within thirty minutes.

After they removed the ventilator, I returned to her room and sat on a cold metal chair. I could see the tape marks on her face. With the ventilator removed, I could see her lips and her nose. I sat quietly with my arms crossed as a wave of anger washed over me. I began to doubt the doctors, and as nurses moved in and out, I was short with them. I wanted to take Jennifer away from all of this, but I clung to the idea that she needed to go to hospice to get better. My dad came in the room to tell me the ambulance had arrived.

I held her hand as she was lifted into the ambulance and continued to talk to her as if she could hear me. I told her I was right by her side. She was unconscious and I was numb, so the drive was silent at first. We drove at a normal pace with no sirens, but inside my heart was racing like a high-speed chase. Clarity and denial pulled at me from different directions, and I gave into each in different ways. In my mind we were going to hospice so that she could improve, yet the words I spoke to her in the ambulance suggest that my heart knew what was happening. I asked her if she was prepared to see Jesus. I expressed my sorrow that she wouldn't be able to see her nephews grow up and that she would never become a mother.

The ambulance stopped and started beeping as it was backing up, but I hardly heard any of it. It was just God, Jennifer and me in that ambulance. Before the driver could walk back and open the double doors, I heard myself whisper to her, "I'm jealous." I don't know why I said it. Maybe it was because I wanted to go with her. Maybe I didn't want to be left alone, without a wife, without a family, and—as I felt at the time—without a future.

I heard the click-click of the lock, and in an instant the doors opened wide. The fresh evening air and the low desert sun rushed towards our faces. It would be our last sunset together.

Once in the hospice center we entered the third room on the left. She was the only patient in the area, but between the staff and all of Jennifer's visitors, the center felt full. Her room had dark green carpet and two twin beds, and they placed her in the bed closest to the window overlooking the courtyard and garden. The nurse came in and explained that Jennifer was very comfortable, that she had extra pillows, and that the position of the bed was correct. Then she discussed how death might take its course, explaining that we should expect unusual breathing as Jennifer's heart was working overtime. The nurse assured me that Jennifer didn't feel anything, and that when death did come, it would be peaceful. She said it could take a few days for her heart to stop beating completely.

I sat in a chair in the room and peered over to the pictures on her end table. Gratitude mysteriously filled my heart in place of the fear and anger I had been feeling that day. *What a wonderful woman. What a wonderful wife. Thank you, Lord, for bringing her to me. Accept her with open arms and let me join her when it's my turn.*

The day stretched on and my emotions went up and down like waves in a storm. I tossed between denial and acceptance, hope and heartbreak, faith and despair. After midnight I realized I hadn't slept in over thirty-eight hours, so I reluctantly went home and slept, wanting to be available for Jennifer the following day. I leaned over her and said the three phrases I had been saying in succession every time I left her side. *I love you. Don't be afraid. I will see you again.*

Deuteronomy 31:6

*Be strong and courageous. Do not be afraid or terrified... for the
Lord your God goes with you; he will never leave you nor forsake you.*

The next morning, March 30, I returned feeling remark-
ably refreshed, especially considering I had only slept three
hours. My parents drove me, recognizing that while my spirit
may have been refreshed, I was probably still a danger to
myself and any other driver on the road with me.

Visitors were coming at a steady pace even before I
arrived. They all looked at Jennifer full of compassion, sadness
or discomfort—for some, maybe, a mixture of all three.
Jennifer could say nothing to them, and I'm sure some felt
like they were too late for their presence to matter. But it mattered to me, and in my heart I know it mattered to Jennifer.

At lunch time I had what I assumed to be some sort of
dull, long-lasting panic attack. I couldn't eat or drink, and
when I talked with family and friends, I couldn't focus on
the conversation. When one of my closest friends asked if
I wanted to go to lunch, I said, "No, I'm not ready to sleep
yet."

"What are you talking about?" he asked.

"I'm not ready to sleep," I said again. "Why don't you
understand that?"

My stress level was at its highest, and I was scared. I didn't
want to leave her side for a moment. When I was forced to

leave in order to go to the bathroom, I would repeat my parting mantra. *I love you. Don't be afraid. I'll see you again.* I said this to her time and again, until I started to take the works to heart myself. Everything was in place; everything was right. I was spending almost every moment by her side, so if she passed while I was away, I knew there would be a reason.

Late that afternoon Jennifer's breathing pattern started to change, going from a normal rhythm to a light pace. She started to moan as if she was having a nightmare, and I was haunted, horrified. The nurse assured me that she wasn't in pain, but the sound frightened me. When it became a constant sound, I had to excuse myself from the room.

"It sounds like she's in pain," I told the nurse.

"Her body is slowing down," she explained. "Her breathing will slow and her body will become cold to the touch." Then she told me I needed to go out and eat.

A couple of my close friends offered to take me out to dinner. I declined at first but felt I had come to a testing of my faith in the words I had been telling her over and over. Was there anything to fear? Would I not see her again? "I love you very much. Don't be afraid. I will see you again," I said to Jennifer, and then I left.

My friends took me to a local joint near the hospital to eat. At 6:12, I looked at my watch and asked for the bill. As we were waiting to pay, a phone call came through. Jennifer had died.

I got out of my seat at the restaurant, walked to the

bathroom, and immediately threw up in the sink. I cleaned everything up and walked outside where I threw up again all over my shirt and pants. I got into the car, numb to the extent of the embarrassment I normally would have felt in that situation, and we rode back to the hospice in silence.

I passed through a group of family and friends on my way to her room, where I knelt next to her body and sobbed over her for several minutes. For comfort, I reached for my leather-bound Bible.

I remembered Hezekiah 20:1, when God instructs Hezekiah to put his house in order and prepare to die. I began to see the blessing in cancer—the chance we'd had to put our house in order and draw near to the Lord together. Others receive a different kind of blessing in death, such as the chance to die quickly with their last years untainted by sickness and pain. But this was our blessing, and I received it.

I turned back toward Jennifer's silent, still body, and I knew she was no longer there. She had done everything asked of her; she had believed until her last breath. I imagined Jennifer walking into the presence of God. I imagined Jennifer's grinning face as she saw Jesus. I imagined them dancing together, her eyes sparkling from the sight of who now stood before her.

CHAPTER 8

The Next Page

April — June, 2009.

ON APRIL 2, 2009, I pressed my suit and wrote a speech, even though I knew I didn't want to say anything at the funeral. My mom asked if I would say a few words, and I responded simply with, "No. I can't." I didn't have the strength or power to do it; I knew there was no way I could get up in front of a crowd and share memories of Jennifer. I also didn't think I needed to share my grief with anyone— it was mine and mine alone. I was looking for a way out and hiding behind anything I could come up with that sounded legitimate.

In the end I wrote the speech because I knew that even

though I couldn't read it aloud, I needed to process what I *would* say if I had been strong enough to do so. I wrote it for Jennifer and no one else.

My shower that morning was rejuvenating, calming, emptying and filling. I found myself smiling while the hot water ran over me. All of a sudden, I knew I needed to speak at Jennifer's funeral. It was as if courage were a room and God's Spirit had just handed me the keys; standing in it, I couldn't imagine *not* speaking that day. Of course I would honor her in that way. I put on my suit and determined that I would go to Jennifer's ceremony with a spirit of celebration for her life. Driving to the church for the service was the first time I had driven myself in over a week.

The church was unlocked but empty. I was the first one there, and I prayed at the altar and prepared myself for what was ahead. I felt the words in my pocket growing heavy and my courage growing dimmer with the emotions that were flooding me. The flowers and casket arrived, and I opened the casket to kiss Jennifer's face. I took off her "live strong" bracelet and placed it on my wrist. I put her wedding ring in my pocket and tucked a picture of the two of us into the side of the coffin. She was dressed in a beautiful purple dress with a cross around her neck. I kissed her again. *I love you so much. I will see you again.* A slideshow of pictures was streaming as people entered the sanctuary.

My introverted self would have preferred to sit down, but I felt the memory of Jennifer's friendliness prodding me to greet people and thank them for their presence that day. God's Spirit broke through my pain, and in the end I greeted every single person who entered the church. Jennifer had finally managed to do it; she had pushed me out of my seat. I even felt at ease with people—something I had never felt before. Jennifer had always been my teacher and champion, but she had also been my shield. I felt the shield and my fear lower even as the memories of her encouragement continued to push me forward. I realized that I had always attributed my aversion to groups of people to my personality, when really so much of it had been a decision. I could choose to dissolve into myself, or I could choose to look up.

The service started with the pastor talking about heaven and earth, beginnings and endings, and the ways that Jennifer had touched and changed lives.

The pastor then asked me to approach the stage with those who would be speaking. I listened intently, gratefully. Then it was my turn. As I stepped forward, something within my spirit stepped up as well. I looked up and peered at the crowd of people who had gathered—each affected by Jennifer's life and death in some way. It amazed me how many people with whom one life can intersect and touch. I reached for the paper in my suit pocket and began by citing Linda Ellis's poem "The Dash," which refers to the small punctuation mark that appears between one's birth date and death date on a tombstone. I couldn't believe how clear my voice sounded. Normally I have a terrible habit of mumbling, especially when I'm nervous or emotional, but my voice came out crystal clear in that moment.

"When we talk about Jennifer's dash," I continued after the poem, "We talk about her leading two young adults to Christ. Jennifer's dash was about the care and love she had for each family member and friend, each patient she took care of. I want you all to know how much stronger than her own husband she was. How she loved learning the Word of God. How much she enjoyed Wednesday night Bible studies and Sunday evening services at our church."

I looked over the crowd of people listening; I couldn't believe the words were coming out of my mouth. My front row seat, where I had planned to sit for the entirety of this service, was vacant. I kept reading.

"Jennifer was a person who said *thank you* for everything, even in her darkest moments. 'Thank you for washing me. Thank you for rubbing my back. Thank you for my medicine.' She never, ever gave up. She lived strong. She wanted all options to be provided to her at any cost until there were no other options left except Jesus.

"I want to thank her again today for being my wife, for accepting my faults, and for being a constant light of what a child of God should be like.

"After her diagnosis, Jennifer got to experience many different events that God gave her more time for. We visited Hawaii to become scuba-certified. She went on a hike and saw a huge waterfall. God gave her the moment when she was on a ventilator, in her hospital bed and unable to speak, to renew our wedding vows. God gave us those moments!

"She has a non-profit organization named after her now. She loved her mother, admired her father, thought the world of her brother, and adored her nephews.

"When she received her nursing degree, it was one of the best moments of her life. She felt on top of the world after a completed scuba dive, during a sunset, playing piano, or sitting on the beach quietly while listening to the ocean waves.

"I thank God she entered my life in high school. I thank God for my marriage to Jennifer. I thank God she was the best thing in my life. I will see you again. I will live my life to become a better man because of you.

"Jennifer, you always wanted to take piano lessons. You are now.

"Jennifer, your dream was to visit Alaska and Australia. Instead, you get to call out on streets of gold.

"Jennifer, you wanted to become a mother. But God had his plan for you.

"Jennifer, you always wanted to go skydiving and take flight lessons. Now you will fly higher than any plane and fly forever without having to stop.

"I will love you for all my days.

Thank you, Jennifer. Thank you, Lord."

As I walked down the stage and took my seat in the front

row, I immediately regretted not sharing a Bible verse. I thought back to Jennifer's first page, when she asked the group gathered around her to share their favorite Bible verses—surely she would have wanted me to share one at her funeral. Then I remembered the verse Jennifer shared that day, Philippians 4:13: "I can do all things through Christ who strengthens me." I knew it wasn't my strength that had carried me through that day, or that held my voice and gaze. Maybe I had forgotten to share a Bible verse, but I had just lived a testimony of Jennifer's favorite.

I rode to the graveside in eerie silence. It struck me that there was no music underscoring the moment as there would be in a movie. When we pulled to a stop, I didn't want to get out. She had already died, but this seemed like another and even more final end. I prayed again for strength, determined to finish strong as she had.

Her graveside was a beautiful spot with a small olive tree. It was perfect.

I took my seat in the front row under the canopy, but the hot April day was making me sweat under my suit, even in the shade. My tears started to fill the bottom inner part of my sunglasses, so I took them off. As the coffin started to lower into the ground, I kept waiting for a director to spring from his chair and yell, "CUT!" But there was no such command, as this was no movie. Jennifer went further, further into the ground.

As the group sang "Amazing Grace," I looked up

through a small break in the canopy ceiling. The son was hot on my face and I could see the blue sky. The day's events were over and a new chapter of my life had begun.

That night I laid my head down on my parents' couch and whispered, "I miss you already." It had been the longest day of my life.

My parents insisted that I stay with them for two weeks; I felt like they were watching me the entire time. It would be a lie to say the thoughts they were worried about didn't cross my mind, but my promise to God and Jennifer kept me from doing anything destructive in my grief.

***

I don't subscribe to the local newspaper, but I knew the April 3, 2009 edition was one I needed to purchase and keep. Still in shock from the preceding days, I had taken on the task of writing Jennifer's obituary. I wanted people to read about the person she was and what gave her joy, not just the fact that she had died of cancer. To my surprise, I wrote only one draft, and it was one I thought Jennifer would have been proud of.

Before I put down the newspaper, I read the other obituaries. I felt connected with the families who had written the pieces, knowing that all of our lives were changed by death on nearly the same day. Most of the people who died were much older than Jennifer, but one story stood out to me. An eleven-year-old girl died in a car accident in our city—I remembered seeing footage of it on the news. The parents had learned that the car their daughter was riding in smashed into a concrete barrier, head-on. My heart broke for their loss, and for the fact that they were never able to say good-bye. She never had the chance to grow up, to date, marry, or pursue a career. Jennifer had been blessed with all of those opportunities. It had seemed so unfair that Jennifer had to leave before the chance to raise children or grow old, but the opportunities she was given were truly a gift.

As for that little girl, I think of her often. I remember her by name in my prayers, and I ask Jennifer to take her by hand.

***

The two weeks at my parents' house passed like a slow-motion roundhouse kick. I needed to go home and be alone. But the house Jennifer and I had shared was now one of the most frightening places in the world for me, and I was absolutely petrified to return.

Even though everything was as I left it, the house seemed completely stark when I returned. Jennifer had always filled that house; without her, there were simply items. None of our things held any meaning for me now. My parents came in behind me, and I took my backpack to the bedroom. Underneath my clothes and toiletries, I found a stack of papers—her seven pages. I sat down and read them for the first time, and all of the memories of those days with her came flooding back with each remark. I tucked them away in a safe place. I needed something meaningful of hers that I could return to over the days to come.

I slept on the couch and used the second bathroom at first. On the fourth night, I ventured into our bedroom, hoping I could conquer my fear and reservations. But I just couldn't do it. I slept on that couch for two weeks before I could finally sleep in bed. When I did, I felt like a little kid afraid of monsters under the bed, closing his eyes in hopes that they won't find him. But I was afraid of the monsters in my head, and usually those get worse when you close your eyes. I thought that I would have hallucinations or muscle memories of swinging my arm around Jennifer's back; but the memories stayed at bay once I settled in, and I slept.

I didn't know what I planned to do with the house, but I knew I needed to remove Jennifer's things from it. Family came over to help me sort through her clothes and items. Soon her dresser stood empty as did half of the closet, which I knew I'd never be able to fill. The next day I called the bank and told them that I could no longer stay in the house; I was ready for it to be foreclosed. They told me just to make my payment and that everything would be all right. They didn't hear. They didn't understand. I would live there almost nine more months, but it never really felt like home again.

***

One of the vows I made to myself was to never again see or enter the hospital where Jennifer spent her last few days. There were certainly many incredible memories from those days, such as our vow renewal and Jennifer's writing of the seven pages, but I held a grudge against this hospital. My wife had entered alive and left barely breathing. I told my parents that if anything ever happened to me, they should take me to a different hospital.

My father called me on April 23, less than a month after Jennifer's death, to tell me that his mom's health was failing. By the sound of his voice, I knew it was serious. He gave me the address to the hospital where I should meet him. I was coming from a different part of town and was talking on my phone, which preoccupied me. But as I pulled into the visitor lot of the hospital, I realized what was happening. I ended my conversation abruptly and reluctantly inched toward a parking spot where I sat in silence. *Why are you doing this to me?* I cried out to God. *I told you I would never come back here. Why here?* I sat with my truck in idle, preparing my excuses. *I'm too fresh out of this experience,* I told myself. *I'm just not strong enough.* My reason pushed against my excuses. *This is your grandmother. You've adored this woman your entire life—you have to go in.* I put the truck in park and turned off the engine. I slammed the driver's door, rattling the mirror. I was just plain mad. I was mad at God for putting me in this spot. I was mad at my family for choosing this hospital out of all the hospitals in Phoenix. I remembered that this was actually the hospital where I had been born. Good grief—didn't Phoenix have any other hospitals?

I decided I would stay for five minutes, say my goodbye,

and leave as quickly as possible.

I asked the woman at the front desk for the room number, and she wrote it on a yellow sticker. I headed toward the elevator. *Here we go again*, I thought, stuck in a dismal kind of *déjà vu*. The moment the elevators opened to floor eleven felt like a kick in the gut, and I looked around, unable to believe what was happening. I glanced down at the sticker again to see the number 1106 (eleventh floor and sixth room)—right next door to Jennifer's 1107.

This isn't happening.

I was so overwhelmed that I couldn't see straight, and I started to cry as my uncle caught sight of me. "This has got to be hard, James. We were here just a month ago," he said. I told him what I had gone through in the parking lot, and what a struggle it had been to make my way up here. He was heartbroken for me and said he appreciated my being there.

The urge to turn away was still strong, but I prayed to God that he would take it away. *Give me the power to walk into the room, Lord. I can do this because you want me here right now.* I wiped away my tears, got up from the chair, walked to the phone and called the nursing desk.

"I'm here to see my grandma, Betty," I said into the phone.

"Come in, dear," the voice answered.

The double doors opened and I could immediately see the sixth room on the floor, but I paused near the seventh and peered in. A man in his eighties was laying in Jennifer's bed, alone, his body straight but his face partially facing the door. I stood motionless for a little while, wondering about his story. I saw the shelf where we had placed pictures; there was a set of new framed pictures there now. Life seemed so round and continual in that moment. I knew there was a time for everything, and that this was his time and his room, not Jennifer's anymore. I looked into my grandmother's room. This was her place and her time.

As I walked into the room I saw my two uncles and aunt huddled around my grandma. Her heartbeat was dropping quickly. I felt the Lord had been preparing me for this moment, and that he was waiting to see if I would lean on him for strength. *I can do all things through Christ who strengthens me.* I placed my arm around my uncle and aunt, and looking across the room I saw another uncle was struggling. I made eye contact with him in my attempt to say, "I'm here. I'm by your side." All of them had comforted me in my recent loss, and it was time for me to do the same.

Suddenly an old memory sprung to my mind from the summer when I was twelve years old. I didn't understand its connection with the moment, but I gave into it. My family had been vacationing with my aunt in San Francisco while her husband was on tour with the military. One day my aunt went into labor, and I was the only one home with her. She told me to drive her to the hospital, but I was twelve and didn't know how to drive. I panicked, but she calmed me down and insisted that I drive her. The vehicle was a stick shift, no less, but I got behind the driver's seat, drove through the city, and somehow, miraculously, brought my aunt to the hospital. I stayed with her in the delivery room and witnessed the entire birth. At last the baby was born.

But the baby wasn't breathing.

An incredible sadness came over me, and I reached out to hold my aunt's hand. I remember feeling like I had a strength to offer her that wasn't my own; I remember feeling incredibly mature, standing in that hospital room, having just driven a car for the first time and now a witness to a powerful moment. At the time it was mysterious to me—I had no concept of faith or God. But standing in that room with my family at the end of my grandma's life, I knew where my strength was coming from. I knew where it had come from when I was twelve.

We weren't made to endure the death of a child, the death of a young wife, or even the passing of a mother and grandmother who has fully lived her years. I considered my grandmother—her death was something close to "ideal," as she had lived many good years and was surrounded by family. But my uncle's eyes told me he was having trouble accepting even that. We were made for health and life and eternity. That world is to come; in the meantime, we lean on God and each other. We struggle. We try to understand. We grieve and we hope.

A few minutes later I witnessed my grandmother's last breath. I thanked God for forcing me out of my truck and pushing me past my fears. I knew I was meant to be in that room at that time. I left the hospital knowing I would speak at my grandmother's funeral; I had no doubt that I could honor her in that way. God had already gone before me.

A couple days later I left my grandmother's service feeling renewed in my commitment to build a life that would honor the Lord. The fog I had been walking through since Jennifer's death was starting to clear, and I saw the decisions I had before me. I could continue to follow my depression down its slippery path, giving in to all my fears and doubts and feelings of anger. At the end of that path I saw sin, darkness and despair. Or I could choose to walk this path of grief with God's strength. I could be honest about my sadness but go to the Lord for encouragement and hope. Most importantly, I could choose to help and serve others.

***

Eight weeks after Jennifer's death, I decided to surprise my mom with a trip to our family reunion in upstate New York. My cousins have a lovely spot in the woods, separated by streams and trees. My mom hadn't been able to go the previous few years due to health and finances, and I knew the trip was what we both needed.

The plane ride with my mother was a sweet time of reconnecting with her, and at the moment the plane stopped at the gate in New York, I felt my spirit breathe. I remember driving through the backwoods and smelling the fresh air. The desert of Arizona has its own beauty, but my soul drank up the trees, the rivers and the small-town vibes of upstate New York. Our family was thrilled at our surprise arrival; they hugged us and took our luggage and welcomed us into their home. After lingering over dinner and a bottle of wine, we went to bed, excited for the following day's games and festivities.

The next day we played games, walked down to a stream, and took a trip up the road to visit a summer camp. Later in the afternoon, iced tea in hand, I spotted a man I didn't recognize, and I surprised myself by automatically walking over to introduce myself.

"Hi, I'm…"

"James, I know. My name's Mike."

He knew my name? I learned he was a neighbor and a close friend of my cousins, and we exchanged pleasantries and talked about the reunion. Then he caught me off-guard.

"I was sorry to hear about your wife," he said.

Over the previous eight weeks I had been surrounded with people who knew me. Mike, however, was the first stranger who acknowledged my loss.

"Thanks, Mike," was all I could manage.

"I know it's tough for you, but you'll get through it," he said.

I felt myself jerk a little at those words. *He has no idea how I'm feeling.* I turned my attention to the kids playing in the front yard and then looked back toward Mike. A gold necklace glistened around his neck, and I took a step to the right just to get out of its reflection.

"Nice necklace," I commented, benignly.

"Thank you. My wife gave it to me. Her name was Beth—she passed away recently as well." My heart stopped at his words. "I wanted to talk with you because I know what happened with Jennifer," he said.

I felt like the patio deck had just shifted in its concrete foundation, and I had to straighten my legs to gain balance.

"I'm sorry to hear about your wife," I said, now part of the real conversation.

"I miss her every day," Mike said. "I try to stay busy as much as possible."

Mike was in his mid-fifties, and even though our lives didn't intersect in any other way, it amazed me how strongly our experiences could connect us so quickly. We chatted a little more and agreed to catch each other later in the evening.

After the sun had set, I grabbed a drink and walked in the direction of laughter and campfire smoke. The ultra-clear moon lit my path in the open woods, giving off an ethereal, calming effect. I sat by the fire with my family as we talked and laughed and made s'mores. One by one, people started turning in for the night, until it was just Mike and me at the fire. Was he waiting for me or was I waiting for him? I switched chairs to be closer to him and decided to start the conversation boldly.

"Do you think you will see Beth again? Do you believe in Jesus?" I waited for his response.

"I don't believe in a higher power," he said. "Do you?"

I didn't think about my response—I just started talking, expecting God to guide me. "I do because I've seen him. I saw him today in my family. I see him tonight in the moon, in the campfire, in my breath. I see him every day through the people I love. I see him in everything. Jennifer did, too. She would have loved this place."

We talked long into the night, sharing our hearts and pain and loss. I marveled at how I was able to offer the love of Jesus to him without feeling anxious about how he would receive it, and I realized his mind wasn't mine to change. I just shared my story and my testimony of God's faithfulness, hoping that he might one day see the same love, strength and power waiting for him, like a gift.

***

On the flight home I thanked God for the weekend. I thanked him for the moon and the rivers and the fresh air circulating through my spirit. I thanked him for bringing Mike across my path... I knew our meeting that weekend was orchestrated by God for the good of both of us.

For the moment, peace occupied the place of loneliness I felt without her. I leaned against my window and watched the sun set on the western horizon.

PART II

CHAPTER 1

The Stages of Grief

IN HER BOOK *On Death and Dying* (1969), Elisabeth Kubler-Ross was the first to separate grief into five stages. Having been through them all, her model rings true for me. In the three months between Jennifer's death and my grandmother's death, and in the several months following both, the five stages manifested themselves in my life. If you're grieving, it can be helpful to review and understand these stages, but don't expect them to happen in perfect, sequential order. Some stages I experienced twice in a sort of loop. Other times the succession seemed very methodical and by-the-book. Of course while I was in each stage, it was anything but method and theory. It was real.

Stage One: Denial and Isolation

It isn't going to happen. It didn't happen. You'll find yourself thinking and feeling these things as if your brain is incapable of wrapping itself around the truth, and you might try to isolate yourself from people and places that shock you back into reality. For most people, this should only last a few days or a few weeks. But for some people, the weeks turn into months, and they get stuck. I think it would have been easy for me to isolate myself had my friends and family not made it so difficult. Whenever I tried to withdraw, someone was calling me on the phone, or asking me out to coffee, or dropping off dinner. Don't reject your friends' efforts to reach out to you.

It was important for me to find ways to combat the loneliness. Music helped. Stepping outside and listening to the birds helped. Keeping the window shades open was important. In fact, the best advice I can offer for this stage is: Don't shut your window shades. Don't close your door to your neighbor. Don't hide in the back of the house until the doorbell stops ringing. Do not sever communication with everyone. You may feel like you need time to hibernate and be alone with your grief, but watching twenty-one hours of television every day and ignoring your phone is not a healthy way to grieve.

Proverbs 18:1

Whosoever isolates himself seeks his own desire; he breaks out against all sound judgment.

There were certainly times that I did not use sound judgment and tended toward isolation. I didn't want to do anything fun because every activity brought back memories and because I felt like I didn't deserve to feel happy. I gained weight and didn't shave. Running a marathon without any water sounded less strenuous than moving my face muscles into a smile.

If there's an activity you enjoy that both engages your mind and allows it to rest, use that activity as therapy during this stage. If you're a writer, write. If you're a quilter, quilt. If you like puzzles, do puzzles. For me, it was golfing. Picking up a club without Jennifer by my side was hard at first, but it made a big difference once I did. And when I did force myself to smile, I noticed a positive shift in my mood and demeanor.

Stage 2: Anger

This is the stage where seeing other people look happy or hearing anyone talk about mundane things fills you with rage. I found myself filled to the brim with pure, unjustifiable anger—just there all the time, waiting to be triggered. Even the sound of traffic made me angry because it reminded me that people were casually going about their lives, unaware that Jennifer wasn't here anymore. I was angry at Jennifer's disease, as if it were a person who had targeted and attacked her. I was angry at myself for allowing it to happen, as if I'd had power over the entire situation and failed to use it. I poured over my regrets and "should we have…" questions. *Should we have traveled to Mexico or New York for those clinical trials?* Sometimes I even felt inexplicably angry at Jennifer. You might think your loved one is the last person you'd be angry towards, and that could be true. You may exhaust every other person or thing you can be angry towards, and your remaining anger can get funneled toward the person who "left you" (as the non-logical part of your brain may tell you).

The faster you understand where your anger stems from, the faster you can get past your anger and face the real emotions feeding it. Sadness, loneliness, disappointment, emptiness… some of these emotions are even scarier to face than anger, because they are more murky and difficult to dwell in. But you have to feel and experience these emotions before you can conquer your anger.

One of the ways you can productively deal with the emotions feeding your anger is to serve other people. Taking your eyes off yourself and choosing to love someone else is like the strongest form of chemotherapy for your cancerous anger. And unlike our earthly treatments for bodily sickness, love never fails. Love actually roots out and demolishes anger.

Stage Three: Bargaining

Take me instead, Lord.

Give me cancer and take it away from my loved one.

If I never do (fill in the blank here) again, will you just...?

If I stop thinking about suicide, will you take away the pain?

To get through this mind-spinning stage of bargaining, you need to come to a belief and understanding that God loves you far more than you comprehend. He does not delight in seeing you in pain, nor is he smiting you and therefore willing to smite you with something else of your choosing. He is also not doling out punishments for your behavior, nor will he be enticed to bribe you into becoming a better person.

Bargaining with God is unproductive, and the sooner you stop driving yourself crazy with bargains, the better. Choosing to grow and develop as a person is a great way to rip through this stage. If you want to make commitments to stop certain destructive behaviors or to follow a conviction, then make the promise and honor it. Lean on the Lord for strength and use your resources to help you get on the right track. Remember that you can do all things through Christ who strengthens you.

Stage Four: Depression

After denial is no longer possible, after your anger has subsided from its initial strength, and after your bargains have failed, you'll begin to feel your heart go numb. Denial may have numbed your heart a little bit in the beginning, but this kind of numbness has a different depth to it.

Depression following the death of a loved one is the dull, painful space between shock and acceptance.

The deep sadness you'll feel in this stage is very real, but people who have never experienced depression will have difficulty understanding what you're going through. Depression affects every area of your life, but it might affect some areas more strongly. My depression leaked through in my communication with others. I was short, impatient and flat.

Many books have been written, drugs created and methods studied for coping with and overcoming depression. I cannot speak to your situation directly and am not a psychiatrist, so I offer no advice in the realm of medication. For me, I chose not to pursue medication.

What I can offer is my testimony. God has proven to me that while he will not spare me from the pain and trials that come with life on this broken earth, he will always be with me in my pain. Turning my life over to the Lord was what made all the difference in this journey. I invited the Lord into each stage of my grief, but it was perhaps in this stage that I felt him closest. I would fall to my knees and ask him to lift my depression; he would reach down and assure me he was present even in my suffering. I asked him for help each step of the way, and he would lift up my head.

Psalm 121:1-2

I lift my eyes up to the hills—where does my help come from? My help comes from the Lord, the Maker of heaven and earth."

A practical note: When you're depressed, it's important to create a structure to your day and follow it. Making decisions is very difficult when you're depressed. You want to avoid lying in bed and asking yourself, "Should I wake up? Maybe I should go back to sleep. I should get up. I should sleep," and on and on. There are hundreds of small decisions like this to make throughout your day, and it's absolutely exhausting when you're depressed. Make those decisions easier by developing a routine, and then go through the motions of your routine whether you feel like it or not. Just do it.

Remember that depression is part of the bridge between loss and acceptance, so don't beat yourself up for going through it. If you feel weak, that's okay. He's strong. Stay open to your circle of support, use your resources, and lean on the Lord. He will not leave you.

Fifth Stage: Acceptance

Provided you walk through each previous stage, and provided you do not experience a tragic memory loss that erases all recollection of your past, this is the stage of grief that you will live in for the rest of your life.

I have a friend who lost his mother twenty years ago. He still misses his mother and always will, but he has long lived in a place of acceptance. Acceptance allows us to live fulfilling and productive lives instead of the kind of lives we'd be doomed to if grief kept us in one of its previous stages. Acceptance is still a stage of grief, but there is life in it. There is joy and peace and purpose in it.

I have a picture of Jennifer on my dresser. She's smiling in the picture, and I love seeing her and remembering her that way. I have a couple other select items of hers around the house—nothing overwhelming or burdensome, but enough to feel like I'm honoring her memory and the place she will always hold in my life and heart. I will always feel sad when I remember her death, but the joy of the Lord overwhelms the pain. The pain will always be there, but I don't live out of it. Depending on where you are in your grief right now, that may sound impossible, but it's true. There is joy on the other side, and all along, God is with you.

Maybe you feel isolated right now, but you're not. God is with you at this very moment.

Maybe every crevice of your being is filled with anger right now. God is holding you in your anger.

Maybe you're devising all kinds of clever bargains and sacrifices. Jesus sacrificed himself entirely for you; he bargained everything he had for you on the cross. Let him carry your burdens.

Maybe you're depressed and struggling just to wake up and put one foot in front of the other. He's there, too. He's near to the brokenhearted (Psalm 34:18).

Maybe you've walked this journey and feel like you're arriving at some sense of acceptance. This can be the scariest step to take. *What's on the other side? What next?* Maybe your grief has normalized and it feels more comfortable than stepping into the next unknown chapter. Take his hand, put your trust in him, and he'll lead the way.

CHAPTER 2

Practical Pages of Grief

GRIEF WILL COMPLETELY uproot your world until you can hardly recognize it for a while. Grief will blindfold and spin you around a few times, leaving you feeling overwhelmed and disoriented. I've written this chapter out of my own experience to help you think through some responsive and proactive ways to move forward.

Develop a Devotional Life

If you have already developed solid spiritual disciplines such as reading the Bible, praying, worshiping and meditating, continue to delve into these practices as a way of grounding you throughout this season and connecting with the Lord. If these disciplines aren't a part of your daily life, now is the time to start.

Often the most difficult part of forming spiritual disciplines is the guilt we have over not starting sooner. Don't let guilt rob you from a single day of fellowship with the Lord.

I had to deal with a lot of guilt in this area. Jennifer and I had wonderful times in the Word together, but there were also plenty of times that I neglected her requests to study more often. Picking up the Bible reminded me of specific times that she would ask me to read with her and I would watch a game or surf the internet instead. I know I was being selfish and immature, both as a husband and as a child of God, and I regret each instance. Yet when I open my Bible now, I focus on the grace God has given me and how far I've come in my walk with him.

If reading the Bible every day is a new practice for you, consider starting with a devotional Bible or a devotional book. Reach out to a strong Christian friend for some suggestions and accountability. Starting in one of the Gospels or another book of the New Testament is usually easiest. If you focus better in the afternoon or night rather than the morning, simply play some worship music to start your day on the right note.

Practice a Healthy Lifestyle

Taking care of your body is one of the most important and impactful things you can do while grieving, but it can also be one of the most difficult things to do when you're grieving.

Going to the gym and putting forth a lot of physical activity may sound therapeutic to you, or it may sound absolutely impossible. If it's the latter, start with a walk around your neighborhood. Start with a tall glass of water every three hours. Start in the produce department, buying lots of fruits and veggies.

It would be simple if eating were simply about nutrition, but eating is about so much more. Eating is the primary way we sustain our bodies, and there's a lot of emotional stuff that comes along with that act. When you feel so desperately in need of comfort, it's easy to reach for the comfort food. Or if you're dealing with survivor's guilt, you may feel like you don't deserve to eat solid, healthy meals every day. I dealt with both.

If you have a friend who wants to help and support you during this season, enlist him or her as a health partner. You can exercise and even plan meals and healthy snacks together. Having someone to help you make decisions and keep you accountable will only be a benefit.

Personal Items

What should you keep? What should you give away? What should you throw away? What should you display, store or file?

Sorting through Jennifer's possessions was one of the most difficult projects I undertook after her death. Disposable items like makeup and toiletries simply needed to be thrown away, while clothing, purses and shoes needed to be donated. Knick-knacks and memorabilia needed to be given to the right person or properly stored, and of all the items that were meaningful to me, I needed to choose a select few to display.

I put off this task for a while, but one day I realized I just couldn't go on opening my closet every morning and seeing her twenty-two pairs of jeans. Family members came over to help, and by the end of the day we had sorted through her keepsake jewelry and stuffed eleven bags full of clothes.

Once that major task was complete, I knew I needed to go through all of Jennifer's memorabilia. I ended up with three plastic containers full of the most sentimental items, such as graduation pictures, journals and some of her nursing study guides. Everyone saves and stores memories differently, and the amount of memorabilia you'll have to sort through will vary from another person's. Go through all of your loved one's keepsake items and properly store them (or give certain items to people who would appreciate them), and if your photos are in disarray, organize them into albums. These are productive, tangible ways to begin sorting through your intangible memories.

One word of caution: Follow your gut with what to throw away and keep, but remember you can always choose to return to storage and throw out items. You can't get anything back once you throw it away. That doesn't mean that you should keep everything, just that you should hesitate before giving away something that holds a lot of meaning and value.

I faced a difficult decision when considering what to do with our wedding rings. The shock of suddenly being a widower left me confused about what I should do with the symbols of our marriage. Initially I thought I should sell them and use the money to do something helpful for a family member. In the end I decided to keep the rings, which I placed in a small wooden box on my dresser. I appreciate being able to see them, and I know I would have regretted selling them.

Items that hold the most value to you may also be the items that inspire the most grief and pain, but don't be so quick to get rid of them. They may be painful to look at now, but you may be grateful to be able to see and touch them later.

Holidays

The first year without your loved one is usually the most difficult. Surround yourself with people you love, and don't skip out on annual events. If you're mourning a family member or mutual friend, remember that you aren't the only person suffering through this loss, and try to be there for others who are grieving through the holiday season as well.

Each Christmas my family arranges a pot luck and white elephant gift exchange. Jennifer always loved going and playing games and just being together with family. During my first Christmas without Jennifer, I decided on the morning of the event that I was just too miserable and sad to go. I was all set to call and explain that I wouldn't be attending when I suddenly felt clear and convicted about the whole thing. This party wasn't about me. This season wasn't about my grief. Christmas is about the birth of our Lord and Savior, who came and died so that Jennifer could have eternal life in heaven. That was good enough reason for me to get out the door and go celebrate with my family.

Your first holiday without your loved one will be difficult—as will subsequent holidays, though your emotions will grow softer. But participating in festivities and rituals in the midst of your grief is an opportunity to practice the discipline of celebration.

Take a Trip (Alone)

Taking a trip by yourself can help calm your stress and strengthen your emotional well-being no matter what stage of grief you're in. One requirement: no friends, and no family members. Go someplace you've never been before to experience something new. A more nature-focused trip will probably be the most peaceful and reflective; if it were me, I'd choose somewhere next to a lake, like Lake Louise in Canada, or Lake Powell in Arizona. Try to stay for at least two full nights, and bring your Bible and a journal. Bring books you've wanted to read and music you enjoy. Do *not* bring work.

If you've lost your spouse, you may not be accustomed to traveling alone and eating alone. Some people do it all the time for work and are very comfortable with it; others shudder at the thought of asking for a table for one. I was used to having someone across the table, so dining alone was a little unnerving for me at first. Going on a trip is a good time to practice eating by yourself, and it may be easier since you'll feel somewhat anonymous in this new location. Be friendly with the staff, and ask a couple nice questions of your server without commandeering him or her for the whole evening while working. People appreciate being noticed.

As your trip winds down, do something nice for someone else. If your maid service was good, leave a generous tip and a note of gratitude. If you frequented a certain restaurant and got to know a server, do the same for him or her. It's a great way to end your trip.

Maintaining Friendships (and Letting Some Go)

My definition of a true friend is someone who will stick with you through thick and thin. I've been blessed with some incredible friends who helped and guided me throughout my grieving process. Some cooked dinner for me, others called just to check in, and some would ask me out for coffee or to shoot some pool. A few asked me some of the most ridiculous questions just to get me to laugh. While I was depressed and holding back from my friendships, these friends never left or gave up trying to reach out to me. Their consistency and generosity humbles me. It's not easy to be a friend to someone who isn't equally giving to the relationship, but these friends were willing to go the extra mile.

I had another group of friends who weren't up for the task. Most of my friends are under forty, so they're not used to a peer losing a spouse, and they didn't know how to act. There are some friends I never heard from again after Jennifer died. I imagine they were scared to call, let too much time pass, and the relationship just died from there. If you find yourself in a similar situation, don't blame yourself or them. Not everyone is emotionally equipped to deal with a friend's loss, and it can be a very difficult and awkward thing to walk through. Friends may be afraid that they'll say something wrong or hurt your feelings in some way, which reminds me: people *will* say the wrong thing and maybe even hurt your feelings sometimes. Don't take every opportunity to correct them, and practice letting things roll off your back. They're probably trying their best.

If you have some friends in this camp who you really don't want to lose, you may need to be the first to reach out. Let your friend know that the relationship is important to you and that you don't want to lose it, even though you probably won't be the best or most thoughtful friend during your season of grief. This may break the ice and put your friend at ease about talking to you.

Most likely you'll realize that not all of your friendships are worth your continued investment. Use whatever emotional capacity you have for friendship to reach out to those who have proven to be true and lasting friends.

Financial Responsibilities

Jennifer and I both had good jobs with medical insurance, but the cost of medical care (including the out-of-pocket expenses that resulted from "pre-existing condition" clauses) left me in quite a bit of debt after Jennifer's passing. Everyone's financial situation is different, but if you've suffered the loss of a loved one in your family due to health issues, chances are your finances look very different than they did before.

If you find yourself in a rough spot, swallow your pride and reach out for help. If your family can't assist you, there may be resources available through local nonprofits that may be able to pay your rent, mortgage or medical insurance premiums. Your church may have a fund for this purpose, too. Many hospitals have contingency funds available. Help is out there, but you'll need to ask around to find it.

At work, don't make my mistake and wait to tell your boss your situation. You don't want to ruin your professional reputation by falling behind at work and not giving an explanation for your behavior. Chances are your boss will want to help and will provide grace.

If legal documents intimidate you, enlist someone to help you go through any applicable legal and financial documents to make sure you're on the right track with your finances. Jennifer had a life insurance policy in order, and cashing that check was one of the biggest hurdles I had to jump after her passing. The check sat at my house for four months before I finally worked up the nerve to cash it. Signing the check brought back memories of signing the DNR form… it felt so final.

I finally did cash the check and put it in a small interest bearing account. I didn't touch it for several months until I was clear about what I wanted to do with it. Eventually I paid off my truck and my debts, purchased a mobile home for my parents, and put the remaining small amount into some stocks and mutual funds. Having a financial advisor oversee this process will give you some peace and clarity about your decisions.

Writing

I started journaling while Jennifer was sick, at her urging. I think she sensed I was so focused on her that I wasn't spending enough time reflecting on my emotions during the process. I was having trouble opening up to her in conversation, and she wanted a way to connect with me. So I would journal and she would read.

Writing became the best way for me to reflect and release my thoughts and emotions, and eventually I started writing songs. I had never written a song before in my life, but they just started coming. I wrote songs with such fervor that I could hardly go to the bathroom without humming, tapping and scratching out some lyrics. I wrote at work, in the car and at home. I poured tons of energy and emotions into my songs... all of which are waiting for someone with musical talent to actually sing them.

The songs themselves weren't the point as much as the opportunity to focus on Jennifer, on God, and finally on myself. Writing helped release my stress and provided an outlet for the many emotions I was experiencing.

If you think you don't have any writing ability, you may surprise yourself. You may not be a "writer" by whatever standards people use to apply that label; but if you're literate, you can write. Buy a notebook or portable laptop and take it with you wherever you go. Make sure you have something next to your bed so that you can jot down dreams and thoughts before and after you sleep. Go to a coffee shop just to write. Don't put pressure on yourself to produce any-thing—just see what happens.

Dating

If you lost your spouse, the dating scene may seem like a very far away, scary place. It's so difficult to pin-point the right time to begin dating again, and it's different for every person. Try not to get hung up on what other people think is appropriate—whether they're pressuring you to start sooner than you want or raising an eyebrow if you're starting sooner than they think you should. Really, the decision is en-tirely up to you.

I went on my first date three months after Jennifer passed, and I'm sure some of my friends and family members thought I didn't wait long enough. But it felt right to me. I wasn't looking for a girlfriend or wife, but I was looking to feel connected and social again.

The first few dates went well enough, but I didn't find any real connection with anyone. Some of them were quite awkward, like when one woman asked me how I could afford to eat out when I wasn't working. Another had the nerve to ask how much I got out of Jennifer's life insurance policy—needless to say, I did not ask her on a second date. There was one woman who I felt attracted to and who was a good conversationalist, but when it came time to taking a deeper step emotionally, I just couldn't do it. I was still too fresh in my grief to move past the social aspect of dating. I spoke to my pastor about it, and he said, "You'll know when God puts the right one in front of you." *When*, not *if*. Eventually the time would be right and the relationship would be right.

Shortly after that conversation, I went on a date with a woman who seemed to hold the same values and morals as me, which I think is the most fundamental element in a potential relationship. I asked her to meet me at a sushi place at six, thinking that if the date was a dud, I could bow out on account of a fish-induced stomach ache. We ended up talking until the restaurant closed, and after a few more dates, we were officially a couple.

Honestly, it was strange to be in a relationship again so quickly. For the first few days I felt like I was cheating on Jennifer by connecting with another woman in a romantic way, but another conversation with my pastor put me at ease. When I married Jennifer, I vowed to never forsake her so long as we both lived. I fulfilled my vow to her sooner than I planned or hoped, but I did fulfill it. I think I would have had to deal with those emotions no matter how long I waited to start dating again.

One of the obstacles of dating after the death of a spouse is how easy it can be to simply compare every new relationship with the one you lost. That isn't fair to the person you're dating, it isn't fair to your late spouse, and it isn't fair to you. Do your best to overcome that tendency. Another common concern is wondering whether you'll ever be able to love the same way again. The truth is that while I will always love Jennifer, that love doesn't demand mutual exclusion.

For some time there was a philosophy going around anti-dating Christian circles called "emotional purity," which went something like: "If you give your heart to one person, you'll never get that piece of your heart back." I agree that it's important to be careful with your heart and not to offer it up carelessly, but I disagree with the idea that you can't fully love more than one person. That's like saying that if you love your first child with all your heart, you won't have room to love your next one in the same way. Friends of mine with kids admit they even worried that would be true before they had their second. Their love for their first child was so complete and overwhelming that they wondered how they would ever love another to the same extent. But they do! Love expands. Love encompasses. Faithfulness to your living partner is a mutually exclusive activity, but love is not. Your heart can love and love again... it just takes time.

If your date is unaware of your situation, you may wonder when and how to explain. It may be too complicated for some to handle, and it might lend an air of gravity and heaviness to the relationship. That probably won't change whether you say something on the first date or the third, and if you wait too long, it may seem like you were trying to hide something. I think it's best to be upfront, but you can limit how much you talk about that part of your life until there is more trust and relational equity. I told my date about my situation on our first date at the sushi restaurant, and she is still in my life today. She's walked with me throughout my grief. When I eventually told her I loved her, she trusted and believed me. She's been an incredible blessing in my life, and I thank God for her.

Whatever you do, incorporate prayer into your dating life. If it's your desire, pray that God will bring someone else in your life at the right time. Pray before each date, that God would help you stay focused on the other person and be a blessing to that person. Pray after each date, regardless of whether you plan to go on a second with that person. Praying for people you date will help you keep your heart open and outwardly-focused.

Make Room for Fun

Make sure you plan for fun in your life. Guys, hang out with your pals; ladies, make times for your girlfriends. Planning fun events and quick getaways with your friends will give you something to look forward to. Concerts, farmers' markets, film festivals, movie nights, fishing, camping, boating, hiking, shopping, a night away in a nearby town or city… try new things, and make time for the things you already enjoy with people you love.

Dealing with Mundanely Bad Days

Bad things are still going to happen to you, which may catch you by surprise at first. Someone will cut you off in traffic or step ahead of you in line at the coffee shop, or the customer at work will get irate and try to attack your competency. Someone will do or say something careless.

The truth is that outside of your personal circle, people don't know what you've been through. It may seem like there's a sign on your forehead, but there isn't. Life "out there" will proceed as normal, which includes good and bad things. If you remember that bad things will happen to you regardless of what you're going through, you'll be able to handle them more gracefully. If someone is rude to you, remember that person may also be fighting a battle, and try to offer more kindness than you're being offered. A kind answer often does turn away anger and rudeness.

After Jennifer's death, someone smashed my truck window and stole my mp3 player. At first I couldn't believe that someone would have the nerve to break into a widower's truck, but the thief didn't know me from Adam, of course. I just had to throw up my hands and hope he listened to some of my worship music.

Riding the Emotional Roller Coaster

Keeping your emotions in check can be a difficult process after losing a loved one. Know and expect that you may experience waves of various emotions at unexpected times and in unexpected places. You may feel generally numb for a while, or your emotions may feel really close to the surface, ready to spring on you at any time. Give yourself grace and deal with each emotion as it comes. Practice breathing and focusing on something positive, and choose a mantra, like, "I can do all things through Christ who strengthens me," or, "God is good, he is sovereign, and he's got the whole world in his hands." Have this mantra ready so that you always have a positive thought to return to when sadness, frustration or anger surprises and overtakes you.

Seeking professional help can be incredibly beneficial when you're coping with loss. Make sure to research someone who specializes in grief counseling, and consider seeking a Christian counselor.

CHAPTER 3

Your Pages

IF YOU HAD TWO DAYS to live and seven pieces of paper, what would you write?

While I believe Jennifer understood she was near the end, I don't think she had those exact terms in mind when she picked up a pencil for the first time in the ICU. But if our days are numbered, so are our pages. And while many of life's pages are filled with grocery lists and spreadsheets, it's important to take time to write something meaningful and intentional. I'm glad Jennifer had that chance.

I love Jennifer's pages because her essence shines from the words she wrote. Words of love, joy and gratitude are on those pages. Her thoughts, questions and observations each say something about her identity, beliefs and personality. The following exercise is about turning inward for a little while and seeing what you find. It's about trying to get something of your essence down on paper where you can see it.

There are seven simple questions, each with space for three answers. But here's the deal: you have to complete all three answers. Don't write the first two answers that pop into your head and then move on to the next question. The point is to get beyond the easy surface answers and go a little deeper.

Find a comfortable spot, grab something cold to drink, and get started.

Page 1: What do you believe?

I believe:

_____

because:

_____

I believe:

_____

because:

_____

I believe:

_____

because:

_____

Page 2: Who are the people you love and care for most deeply?

I love:

_____

because:

_____

I love:

_____

because:

_____

I love:

_____

because:

_____

Page 3: When do you feel most alive? (Satisfied, content, whole, engaged in life?)

I feel alive when:

_____

Maybe that's because:

_____

I feel alive when:

_____

Maybe that's because:

_____

I feel alive when:

_____

Maybe that's because:

_____

Page 4: Who do you admire?

I admire:

_____

because:

_____

I admire:

_____

because:

_____

I admire:

_____

because:

_____

Page 5: Who do you forgive?

I forgive:

_____

for:

_____

I forgive:

_____

for:

_____

I forgive:

_____

for:

_____

Page 6: What change do you want to see in the world?

I want to see:

_____

I can participate by:

_____

I want to see:

_____

I can participate by:

_____

I want to see:

_____

I can participate by:

_____

Page 7: What do you hope for?

I hope:

_____

I hope:

_____

I hope:

_____

CHAPTER 4

The Eighth Page

HERE'S MY STORY in a paragraph:

I came home from work one day and my wife said the word that changes everything: cancer. I had been coasting through life to that point, taking most things for granted. But I knew I couldn't coast through cancer on auto-pilot. I woke up. It's funny how much clearer things become when you're awake! I opened my eyes to Jesus and found my Savior and King. I opened my eyes to my wife and found the woman I loved, fighting with all her strength. I looked inward and saw a whole mess of things I knew needed to change. Slowly, I did. Every day, I am.

Today I live on the eighth page. Jennifer's seven pages led me to the place where I am today, so I call this—the here and now of my life—the eighth page. It's a place of aware-ness that I am writing on numbered pages and living out my numbered days. Maybe that sounds dismal, but it's the op-posite. When I was living without thought of limits, I wasn't really living life to the full. By acknowledging the limits God has lovingly set for my life, I gained a sense of gratitude and focus. Psalm 16:6 says, *"The boundary lines have fallen for me in pleasant places; surely I have a delightful inheritance."* Psalm 139:16 says, *"All the days ordained for me were written in your book before one of them came to be."*

What about you? Have you started your eighth page yet? Are you present and engaged in the here and now? If your "now" is a place of grief, being present means being fully in your grief and not getting stuck in those first or second stages. If you're further along in your grief and are starting to arrive at a sense of normalcy, being present may mean starting to turn outward, serving others, and taking notice of good and beauty in the world.

Living on the eighth page doesn't mean you can't turn back and revisit memories. Memories—pure, lovely and good ones, anyway—are gifts that we can choose to open whenever we want. But recognize the limitation of a mem-ory and pay attention to whether you're spending more time in the past than you are in the present.

Here's another question. *Are you earning your life?* In one of my all-time favorite movies, *Saving Private Ryan,* a dying Captain John H. Miller tells Private Ryan, "Earn this. Earn it." Many soldiers died to save Private Ryan. His life was a gift purchased by the lives of others. We have been bought, too; Jesus paid the ultimate price to give us the gift of life. Having received that grace before we ever did anything to deserve it, we now have the opportunity to become "worthy of the gospel" and to "work out our salvation" (Philippians 1:27, 2:12).

I feel honored to have witnessed Jennifer working out her salvation in her last days. She never grew weary in her faith, but instead she persevered, always believing, always trusting. The love of Jesus radiated through her sickness and disease. What a testimony!

What's your testimony? *Share it.* Stories are meant to be told, lights are meant to shine, and Jennifer had a story and a light that I wanted to share. What's your story and who needs to hear it? I think you'll find there's a blessing that comes with opening up and sharing your heart with others.

***

Visiting Jennifer's gravesite has become a ritual of sorts for me. The first time I went was the day after her burial, and I remember how strange it was to see the same tent set up about seventy-five yards away for another service. I stood next to the small olive tree and looked at the little plastic dolphin sitting right above the "J" in her name. Purple lilies peeked out of a bronze vase on top of the clean stone. I knew my life would never be the same.

Now when I visit her gravesite, I sit in the grass and cross my legs. I open my Bible and wait for the Lord to calm my nerves and fears—he always does. I open to Philippians and begin with Jennifer's favorite verse, then move to another chapter and read.

I also play music, and I always begin with the same two songs. One is by Jeremy Camp called *There Will be a Day*. I listen to it and imagine where she is and where I'll someday join her: a place with no tears or pain. Knowing that Jeremy Camp also lost his young wife to cancer adds a lot of meaning to the song for me, because I know he's singing from a similar place of grief and hope. The other song I listen to is *Call My Name* by Third Day. I met the members of Third Day in Phoenix at an autograph signing event, and I told them pieces of Jennifer's story. Two of the band members stopped what they were doing and prayed with me, right in the middle of the hustle and noise and flashing cameras. It was one of those moments when everything fades into the background and I could feel God present and at work.

I trust and ask God to give me a long life so that I can serve him and bless others. But I know "There Will Be a Day" when he will "Call my Name." I want God to find me serving and loving him with all my soul, heart and strength. His grace is a free gift, but I don't ever want him to find me apathetic about it.

Jennifer and I share the same gravestone. It's a moderately large stone with a bronze outline of hands folded in prayer at the center. Her name is followed by a birth date and death date, while mine is followed with a birth date and a dash—just hanging there, waiting for completion. For the longest time I couldn't look at it without feeling anxious and a little afraid. My birth date is set in stone and the dash is so short. Other questions (like what would happen to the stone if I remarried) used to plague me when I looked at it. But now I try to focus on the positive aspects of getting to see the dash on my grave while I'm alive. I ask constructive questions, like: *What am I doing to improve and better myself? What am I doing to serve and help others? What steps am I taking to deepen my relationship with God?* These are the questions I want to be working through now, in my dash.

How about you? Have you visualized and come to terms with your dash? What questions do you ask to keep yourself on track?

***

While Jennifer was alive, I looked her in the eye and agreed to four promises. They've been a gift, really, because these promises have provided guidelines for my daily living.

First, I promised Jennifer that I would "never lose faith in Jesus Christ." That's the wording we used at the time, though now I've turned it into a positive statement: "Always keep faith in Jesus." God is constant, but our hearts (as the old hymn goes) are "prone to wander," and we have to choose to hold to our faith. Do we doubt his love and mercy? He is there. No matter where we are, he is always there. God never leaves, and when we wander, he's always there to welcome us back.

Are our prayer-bones too rigid to touch the floor? Remember, "Every knee shall bow and every tongue will confess that Jesus Christ is Lord" (Philippians 2:10-11). Our first step to reconnect with God is to pray. At first I felt like it was silly to get on my knees, but that was before I discovered God as my Father who gave me life.

If you don't know what to say, your first prayer can be a request for words. "Lord, teach me how to pray" is a great way to start. Present your feelings, fears, and thankfulness to him. He can hear us and wants us to talk to him. You will be amazed at how your prayer life can transform your daily life. If you've never read the Bible, ask someone who has and who believes in it. It is a transforming book if you will let it enter your heart. Don't try to reason it out, because it is not intellectual property but rather spiritual property. That doesn't mean it's illogical or nonsense... it just means that you'll have to use a wider range of tools than mere intellect to understand it. Ask questions and be ready to listen.

The second promise I made to Jennifer was that I would become successful.

If that sounds like a strange or selfish promise, then you probably have a different definition of success than we were using. To us, the best success we could imagine would be to make a difference in the lives of others by serving, helping and uplifting. Whether our impact was small or large didn't matter; what mattered more to us was the quality and the trajectory of the impact rather than the scope of it.

Most of us want to live successful lives, but if our idea of success is something monetary, material or status-related, our success will always be something that the world can take away. Also, if you die before you achieve those things (or if you achieve them *and* see them taken away), your life will not be a success by your own definition.

There's nothing wrong with earning money and having goals for your career. But your definition of "success" should be something eternal… something that can't be taken away. It should be something that you can achieve today in some small way and that you can continue to build and pursue for the rest of your life.

The third promise I made to Jennifer was that I wouldn't be afraid to remarry and raise a family. The greater promise here was that I wouldn't get stuck in the wake of her death. I wouldn't let it halt me from living the life God had for me.

Finally, I promised that I would live a life that would honor God.

What could have gone unsaid in that promise—but which she made sure to say anyway—was this: in order to live a life that pleased God, I would have to choose to live. I went to some dark places following Jennifer's death, but this promise kept me going strong even when the easier thing to do would have been to give in and give up. I'm here today, living on my eighth page, by the grace of God and by the power of a promise.

Psalm 23

The Lord is my shepherd; I shall not want. He maketh me to lie down in green pastures: he leadeth me beside the still waters. He restoreth my soul: he leadeth me in the paths of righteousness for his name's sake. Yea, though I walk through the valley of the shadow of death, I will fear no evil: for thou art with me; thy rod and Thy staff they comfort me. Thou preparest a table before me in the presence of mine enemies: thou anointest my head with oil; my cup runneth over. Surely goodness and mercy shall follow me all the days of my life: and I will dwell in the house of the Lord forever. (King James)

CHAPTER 5

Seventh Heaven

IT DIDN'T OCCUR TO ME until I nearly finished writing this book how often the number seven occurs throughout Jennifer's story.

Seven AM – seven PM: Jennifer's shift at the hospital

Seven feet: The depth of the pool where I prayed on the raft

7/07/2007: The day we had "The Conversation." (We discussed for the first time the real possibility of her death, and I made the promises she asked me to keep.)

Room seven: The room where we discussed treatment options with the incompetent doctor

Seven attempts: The number of times Jennifer was

pricked with a needle in an attempt to find a vein for her first IV

Room seven: Jennifer's room on the eleventh floor of the ICU

Seven pages: The number of pages containing Jennifer's last words

Many from the Judeo-Christian faith believe that the number seven symbolizes spiritual perfection or completeness. The seven days of creation is one biblical example, complete with God's stamp of approval, "It was good." Jesus told his disciples that we must not forgive someone a mere seven times, but rather "seventy times seven"—in other words, until we have perfectly forgiven. "Lucky number seven" is derived from these and many other references to the Bible, which worked their way into mainstream conscientiousness.

Some would say the number seven is just a number and nothing more. And it's true that there is nothing inherently magical or mystical about the number seven. It doesn't have the power to do anything or bring us good luck. But when we read literature, we look for symbolism and foreshadowing and themes because we know the author uses those devices to convey meaning. In the same way, I believe Jesus—the "author" of our faith—often weaves signs and messages into our living stories.

A seven-to-seven nursing shift isn't unique, and if the

number seven hadn't repeated itself in so many other ways, I never would have given it second thought. But now when I consider Jennifer's shift at the hospital, I'm reminded that God was with her as she shined her light during those moonlight hours. When I was on the raft in seven feet of water, I was head to toe in his grace. On 07/07/07, a day that thousands of couples were having their weddings in hope of scoring some luck, God was present as we had our pivotal conversation. The fact that the incompetent doctor met with us in room number seven is of particular significance to me; even when we felt discouraged, angry and disappointed, God was still with us. (Again, the room number doesn't validate that fact, but rather reminds me of it.) When Jennifer was getting repeatedly poked with needles for her first IV, the seventh attempt was successful. God was present in room seven in the ICU. Her seven pages were complete, capped off with: "I want to go home" on the seventh page.

Jennifer's seventh page stands as both a comfort and a challenge to me. I am comforted to know that my wife found peace before death, and I'm comforted that her soul recognized and longed for the home she would find beyond life here on earth. But her words have an edge and a challenge to them. Am I ready to be called home? Am I living each of my days for the glory of God? Does my soul rest in the assurance and security of God's eternal love?

God continues to place me in situations that remind me how swift and delicate our physical lives are. In the final weeks of writing this book, I witnessed a horrific motorcycle accident. I pulled over and ran to the young man who had been thrown from his bike, and I immediately held his hand and began to pray. For several minutes I sat there with him, trying to take his pulse, holding his hand, praying, praying, praying. I continued to pray out loud, on my knees, even as the EMT staff started to arrive.

The young man was pronounced dead on the scene, and the police told me to go to trauma counseling at the police department before going home. I sat across from the grief counselor, crying about what I had just witnessed, when she suddenly began to cry, too. Her husband died in a motorcycle accident a little over a year ago, she explained, and she didn't know if anyone held his hand.

I don't know why I was placed in that situation, or why this particular counselor was on shift, but I know it happened for a reason. I'm learning this is true of everything in life. I don't know why so many things that happen, happen. I haven't a clue. But what I am absolutely confident of is that there is a reason and a purpose behind it all. Even the senseless, unfair and evil things in this world are being woven together in a purposeful way. We can choose to rail against the tragedies of life and call them meaningless and wasteful, or we can choose to grieve while holding onto the only hope that anchors our souls: the hope of Jesus.

My prayer for you is that you find and hold fast to that hope. May doing so draw you deeper into the full, meaningful life you were given to lead in Christ, and may it urge you to look outward toward the lives you are here to impact and serve.

CPSIA information can be obtained at www.ICGtesting.com
Printed in the USA
LVOW08s0035130514

385446LV00004B/408/P

9 780996 036177